MEMORY AMBERS

SATYAPAL ANAND

Trafford rev. 05/26/2016

 www.trafford.com

North America & international
toll-free: 1 888 232 4444 (USA & Canada)
fax: 812 355 4082

CONTENTS

Reflections and Reminiscences

All about My Children

Of Persons and Personalities

The Last Naughty Piece

For my children
Pramod, Daisy and Sachin
Simmi and Bina

AN INTERVIEW WITH MYSELF

Who will ever think of interviewing someone who has interviewed others scores of times? Reflecting on this tragicomedy of a man – no other than myself –I thought of putting some questions to the second *self* of me which is *not me*. The difficulty arose when *not I* had any knowledge of *me* in first person pronoun *per se*. So I reversed the roles and let *not me* ask all the questions.

Not me ☺ **(interviewer):** Dr. Anand, what is the logic behind this title, *Memory Ambers*? Re-enkindling memories, good and bad … why are both kinds placed in the painful category?

Me: ☹ **: (interviewee):** An amber is defined as a 'yellow or transparent fossil resin formed along some sea coasts and used as jewelry. It is hard, easily polished and quickly electrified by friction.' So are these written pieces. To me this word denotes much more than a mere piece. It is a hard piece of some story substance, as you put it, electrifying you … mildly, of course, like giving you a mild shock..

Not me: ☹ But, why?

Me:☹**:** The best way to forget an alarming memory, say the *pundits* of psychiatry, is to remember it first. Savor its bitter-sweet taste once again. Relish it. Lick your fingers, if you like it, but never spit it out. I have done that.

Not me☹**:** Mr. Anand, OK. Let me ask another question now. ..How is it that you have started writing and publishing more in English than in Urdu, a language that was your *forte* for more than half a century?

Me ☹ I am afraid that is a question to which I have a ready answer. Firstly, I did not stop writing in Urdu; I just cut it down

1

to its size in the reservoir of my mental and physical capacity. You see, except for a few hundred – or maybe, a few thousand modern poetry enthusiasts more in Pakistan than in India, no one *ever* found a *vernacular* writer worthy of notice, while writers in English reaped – and are still reaping - the rewards of name and fame in both these countries. Besides, I had been writing in English even while my main field was Urdu. Well, now I have both, side by side. It is like having a wife and a concubine on the same bed with you, or on both sides of you. How do you like this comparison?

Not me☺: Well, I don't like it because not only even general comparisons are always odious but those between moral and immoral entities are more so. . If I put another question, you might have to explain which language is your wife, thus automatically giving the status of a concubine to the other? So, I let it be. Is there any other reason?

Me☹: besides, there is no money in it at all.

Not me☹: You mean, no one gets paid in Urdu?

Me☹: Well, maybe some still are paid but I am not one of them. Well, there was a time when I was also paid, say a hundred rupees for a short story, but that was in the fifties of the last century. Now, the position is in reverse. Not only Urdu publishers don't pay to the authors, they expect the author's to fray the total cost of the publication of the book – and for their help in getting it published, they retain any number of copies, a hundred or a few hundred free of cost for selling themselves....Let me share a secret with you. I have more than a dozen books published by a Delhi publisher and Pakistani editions of three of them are published from Karachi. My total royalty from these books is *nil*. Repeat *nil*. The publishers' notion is that publishing an author's book is an act of social philanthropy ... and a personal favor too. So they don't pay.

Not me☹: And the readers in Urdu?

Me☹. Readers, did you ask? I don't understand, my dear, what readers? Are there any? Some there are, of course, that buy books but, by and large, not even one in ten thousand of our countrymen read. And this includes men and women of all classes, the super rich, the rich, the upper middle class, the middle class ... and you keep on descending these stairs till you reach the slave workers – or working slaves. Of course, some are there who read film magazine and adolescents, particularly in Pakistan, buy media poets' works that contain love poetry. There are no serious readers, my dear.

Not Me☹: I agree, but did writing in English bring you quick money?

Me☹: Well, not much, but even a small check would be welcome when you know that Urdu and Hindi are but dried up cows.. Look, shall we talk about *what* I write rather than *why* I write?

Not Me☹: Well-answered Sir; Will you mind if I address you as Sir now?

Me☹: Yes, I will.

Not Me☹: O. K. Then, I will not insult you by addressing you as Sir. I do know a little bit about *what* you write. Poetry, of course, both in English and Urdu is your *forte*. What about this book? It is not poetry: It is a hold-all of all of your literary baggage in English prose. Pieces and parts, specimens and slices, chips and sips – indeed, all kinds of prose are there. Satire, both sarcastic and sardonic is there. Personal memoires, both delightful and disturbing are also there. A tongue-in-the-cheek approach is about Urdu-wallahs' scatter-brained writing. What else can you say? Haven't I summed it up?

Me☹: Yes, but in all 'pieces and parts', as you call them, have that uncontrollable quality of a clicking tongue in a reddening cheek. I disrobe everything and everybody. I don't spare the small fries who act as Goliaths. I think, in this collection, the only person I have written about with unadulterated admiration bordering on reverence is His Holiness the Dalai Lama.

Not me☹: Yes, I understand.... But what is so special about you? There are many of us who can guffaw at a funny story, at a limerick, or at a pun. (*What was Joan of Arc made of? ... She was Maid of Orleans*). Why is your humorous writing so special?

Me☹: I don't know. Could it be that I use first person pronoun as a narrator in all my 'chips and sips' as you call them in your

3

colorful parody? Telling a story in first person is not a formula for success in writing comic pieces, unless of course, one makes oneself the butt of ridicule. The laugh is on the author, you see, and he doesn't mind acting the proverbial fool … Falstaff or Sir Toby … or even Khoji of Ratan Nath Sarshar's *Fasana-e -Azad.*

Not me: Yes, but what about non-humorous tidbits?

Me☺: You see, the personal-parody type is a civilizing attempt to put some order in the jungle of the mind of all readers. Which of us, who is given a column to write for a newspaper, and who sets out happily to fill it with accounts of his domestic adventures, unless he is writing about his friends? This, of course, is the cult of the Columnist as a Fool. But I do not indulge in this luxury all the time. I have very serious pieces that have adorned the pages of a galaxy of literary magazines.

Not me☹. I see, you do have quite a variety. I do see the scholar in you standing apart from the clown in you.

Me☺: You know, being *Not Me* you have the uncanny ability to divine the nature of my words before I utter a single syllable. Yes, the scholar in me often stands at a distance and pooh-poohs the joker in me. This is a kind of writing that is not on the shelves of the drugstore of humorous writing. There are, of course, clowns of the suburbs in Urdu columnists, I dare say, particularly some in Pakistan. Their creed is simple. What is the use of being wise if you are not sometimes merry? The merriment of men is not the uninformed, gross fun of ignorant men, but it has more kinship with that man who has pinched look, who is frightened and cowering under the shower of words from the wise.

Not-me☹. What about really serious, let's say, just short-short remembrances of things about your students or colleagues? Aren't these a category apart?

Me☹: Yes, I agree with that summation. These write-ups show the softer side of my approach to men, manners, and matters – indeed – in these pieces I am not myopic at all. I am all feeling, all emotion, all sympathy ….

Not-me☹: Well. I think it is well nigh enough for one sitting. Shall I say it was a pleasure to talk to you? ... I mean it was your pleasure in talking to yourself.

Me☹. I agree but what I said about myself was an example of my art of masochistic self-parody: indeed, it was not self-glorification.

Not-Me: Let's have the last nail in the coffin of this interview. Have you decided to write more in English than in Urdu now? (Mark the absence of the laughing icon!)

Me. Well, I don't know for sure, but the way I've started digging the gold mine of my memories, I think I will have to dig up more dirt and experience the self-inflicted pain of many, indeed many more shards that will be collected in the second part of this book.

* * *

Para-Normal Experiences

The very puzzling on the brink
Of what is called Eternity to stare
And no more of what is here, than there.
                                    -Lord Byron, *Don Juan*

PROPHECIES WITHIN PROPHECIES

I believe there's something in predictions of doom and destruction. The truth, indeed, may be just a grain of salt in such prophecies, but even that grain of salt is enough to make you feel uneasy about the future of mankind. We know of Nostradamus (1503-1566), who made many prophecies about the human race which have come true. It is now known that the Italian National Library in Rome made an amazing discovery in May 2005. Buried in their archives was a hitherto unknown manuscript by the prophet of doom that he had handed to his son and later was donated to Pope Urban VIII. It did not surface again until now, almost 400 years later.

Reading through the cutting edge data and deciphering it by *The Nostradamus Code,* this manuscript reveals that 2007-2015 would be the years of widespread war and upheaval in the world. Well, we know what's happening in the world, and if we go by the words of Prince Hassan of Jordan – "I'm afraid the making of the World War III is actually taking place in front of our eyes."

You see, we never perceive of an impending event of death and destruction in political terms. We always think it is going to be natural occurrences like flood or earthquake or plague (Remember the Egyptian soothsayer who had predicted the ten plagues and whose eyes were gouged out by the pharaoh!) Political occurrences somehow remain outside the spectrum of our thought when it comes to prophecies of doom and destruction.

What I am telling you, friends, is truth and nothing but the unadorned truth. It happened when I was 12 years of age, i.e. back in 1942 in Rawalpindi. A Hindu astrologer, known for the veracity of his astrological calculations, discovered just by chance that the celestial conglomeration of planets predicted that *pralaya* (doomsday) was at hand and that within two years it would be on us. He toured the length and breadth of Punjab, lecturing in Hindu temples and Sikh temples foretelling the severity of the events to come. The former Prime Minister of India, Mr. Inder Kumar Gujral's father was a very rich man of Jhelum and he helped him bring out a million copies of a booklet called *Chetawani* (Warning) in Urdu, Hindi and Punjabi for free distribution.

I read that booklet in Urdu. It said that within two years hundreds of thousands of people would be killed; there would be death and destruction all around from Indus to Yamuna and beyond. Nothing could be done about it, the booklet said. The astrologer was so sure of himself that he promised to commit suicide at the end of 1944 if his predictions didn't come true.

There were all kinds of holy *yajnas, hawans* and collective prayers in Hindu and Sikh temples to ward off the calamity or at least to lessen its severity. Heathen that I was even at that age, I laughed outright. Whenever the subject came for discussion in my household, I told my dad and mom that it was nothing but hogwash.

Well, no one could even think back in 1942 that the doomsday might not be a natural calamity but a political upheaval of violent dimensions. People in their millions read the book but never could think in terms of the partition of India. When, finally, the partition came, they had already forgotten about the book, because the astrologer, as promised by him, had committed suicide back on 31st December 1944.

It is a different story, not entirely unrelated, how (according to unofficial estimates) three and a half million people lost their lives on both sides of the border. There was an exchange of populations and millions migrated from one country to the other.

During one of my inter-university seminar engagements, back in 1967 I met a well known astrologer in Madras now known as Chinnai, a metropolitan city in the Southern Indian state of Tamil Nadu. He had never heard of the book Chetawani, and I explained in detail about its contents. He asked me to come over the next day and by that time he would have calculated the star tables. I went the next day. He was beside himself with joy because he was sure to convince a Professor that astrology was not a mad man's dream. He said that he had re-calculated twice and he came to the conclusion that the only reason why that particular astrologer's predictions proved to be wrong was that he had slightly miscalculated and pre-dated the event by two or three years. Since astrologers calculate by lunar calendar and that too in terms of the Hindu *Vikrami Samwat*, even the littlest departure of one or half an hour or, he said, could've taken him off course.

He said: "The astrologers are never wrong; they sometimes inadvertently miscalculate." Then he added, "Don't you agree that the partition and the suffering it caused to millions of people was no less than a *pralaya*", the doomsday? I asked him the crucial question, "Can you try and re-calculate it now?" "No," he said. "I can't and I won't. How can past be predicted? I deal with future and future only."

So, as predicted by Nostradamus, is there going to be death and destruction in the years to come? We've already seen natural disasters like the earthquake in Pakistan. We are watching, with dismay, the daily loss of human life in the Middle East. The President of Iran has said that Israel should be wiped off from the world map. We know that Israel is a nuclear state and if its very existence is threatened, wouldn't it use them? It is not a moot question, my friends. USA did use them against a non-nuclear country, namely Japan, even when the existence of USA was not threatened.

And, finally, what about the new emerging axis of power in Iraq-Syria combined threatened by ISIS, a Caliphate in the twenty-first century swearing by the medieval Islamic laws with ambitions to conquer the rest of the world? Already they have issued a map that includes the entire Middle East, Horn of Africa – down to the middle of the dark continent, one-third of Europe, almost the entire South Asia right up to beyond-the-Himalayas countries of Central Asia, parts of China and Russia. Well, it might be an opium dream, but if they continue to convert that dream into reality through means foul, foul and foul, there is no end to violence. One might think of the hellish scenario if in achieving these targets, weapons of mass destruction are used – not only by the perpetrators of mass-scale violence but also by the defenders.

Don't ask me, friends, if I am still the skeptic that I was when I was 12 years old. I really don't know.

(June 2008)

*   *   *

OUT OF BODY EXPERIENCE

There have been numerous occasions when one comes across, either as a personal experience, or as a re-told actual story by a friend, an experience beyond one's ordinary understanding. "Out of Body Experience" is one such thing. I would not have found it trustworthy but for the fact that I nursed my wife (alas, she's no more!) for over two years when she was in and out of coma for a number of times. I always believed that the grand thing about the human mind is that it can turn its own tables to see meaninglessness as the ultimate meaning. Bertrand Russell in his The Conquest of Happiness says: "The mind is a strange machine which can combine the fact with a fantasy – and when you look at it carefully you might find that fantasy is more fact than fact itself.

It was back in 2004 and my wife was in the hospital fighting for her life after total kidney failure. It was late in the evening and I was in the chair, half asleep, by her bedside.

Suddenly she opened her eyes and called me by my pet name for her: "Jaani!" she said.

I stood up and said, "God bless! You're out of coma!"

She said haltingly in Punjabi, "You know, I was dead for a while."

I was taken aback.

"No, I really was..." she said, "and I wandered in the long corridors and wards and even in the canteen where people were having their dinner."

I touched her on the forehead. It was cold to my touch, not warm and perspiring as I had expected.

Still a little confused, I said, "You must've been dreaming, but thank God you are out of coma. Let me call the nurse."

She closed her eyes and then looked at me earnestly, "No, don't call her. You see, dear, I really was not in my body but wandering about." Then she added after a pause, "Do you know that the patient in the room next to mine is dead already, but even the nurses don't know it. She was also wandering with me."

I was taken aback because suddenly there was a flurry of activity outside. Nurses rushed past my wife's room; there was a hectic discussion on the nurses' phone and someone said a little loudly. "Oh God, she's no more!"

I went out of the room a few steps. The patient next door, an elderly lady, had really died....I came back. My wife's eyes were closed, but she said, "You see, I wasn't telling a lie."

"Yes, dear," I said, "You did go out of your body, but what did you do and how did you come back?"

"Well, I don't know for real, but suddenly I found myself lighter than air. Hovering over my bed, I could see myself lying. Like a breath of breeze, I touched you on the cheek. You didn't feel my touch. Then I went outside; I was walking...no, flying... no floating, ah, yes, floating. I went to the canteen; with the idea to bring a cup of coffee for you....I touched the coffee pot. It wasn't a touch 'cause my hand went through it. I tried to pick up a newspaper for you. Strangely enough, although I couldn't pick one up, the stack was disturbed and some papers fell on the floor. Everyone looked at it, but no one could see me. Then I thought of coming back to the room – and here I was, once again on the bed, with you in the chair, and then I spoke to you and told you that for a while I was dead."

Well, by this time, I had swallowed the whole truth. She really had had – what is called – an out–of–body–experience. But, curious as I was, I asked her again. "And what did the lady next door do? One who had died almost the same time as you had."

"Oh, she?" My wife said, "She wandered alongside me and said something to me. I could see only her lips moving, but there was no sound. Then she went out of the hospital to the parking lot. Maybe, she wanted to drive her car back to her home.".....

I thought she was making a jest of it, but no, she had said it in the right earnest as if she believed that people, who are dead, can drive cars.

*   *   *

ARE WE BORN AGAIN?

Well, I was born a Hindu and so, from my very childhood, I had cultivated the idea of transmigration of souls. In my mature age, I read teachings of two major religions of the world, namely Christianity and Islam – and neither of these two world-wide religions, ever mentioned, positively or negatively, of the claim that human soul, being imperishable, finds a new body for itself every time it leaves its old home, a human body. Buddhism, an off-shoot of Hinduism and Jainism, of course, not only supports the idea in its nascent form but also teaches practical steps to be taken by an individual to get out of this cycle of birth and re-birth.

In my life I have been searching for verifiable answers to this question in books on the subject and in religious texts. Buddhist literature, I have read and re-read to the extent of memorizing some of its *sutras*. So has been the Hindu supreme text *Bhagwad Gita*. However, at least four instances have occurred in my own life where my own eyewitness account will leave my readers with this question 'Are We Born Again' with a redoubled force. Here are all four of them, recapitulated by me as memory shards.

Back in 1963, on the campus of Panjab University, Chandigarh, we had a visiting scholar from Montreal, Canada, an India-born Hindu with a French born Christian wife. This was their second trip as they had got married in India itself about five years ago when the young lady was visiting the country as a tourist. The couple had gone back to Canada to be with the wife's family. A girl was born of the union there. Now when this baby was three years old, they had come to India on a visiting assignment.

Being of the same age, this colleague and I became friendly enough to be on visiting terms. One day he asked me to come over to his house. There he told me that his little daughter, the three-year old Emily, talked in her sleep in a language that sounded like French but they could not understand a word of it. Even in the afternoon while she was asleep, she bubbled out strange words that sounded like complete sentences. She often raises her hands in supplication and cries out," he said.

He thought that the words she uttered were in French, but a jargon that his wife, a Canada born lady of French origin, had never heard before. The baby, he said, was never exposed to anything but English in which the husband and wife conversed. In fact, the baby was learning to speak English rather slowly and although she was about three years old, she could utter only a few babyish words in English for mom and dad and for her toys. "My wife," he told me, "knows a little bit of French but all that we could decipher was that the baby was asking for her mother all the time – in a language that she never was exposed to much less know to converse in."

I was intrigued. I stayed for the day and watched the baby asleep in her crib. At least on three different occasions I saw the baby raise her hands and heard her bubbling forth in French, babyish speech but discernable. "I want my Ma; my Ma I want." She repeated again and again. "Where is my Mummy?" she reverted to English but then again lapsed into French.

We had a gracious old lady who taught short courses in French on the campus. Mrs. Bool Chand (pronounced *Ma'am Bool Shan*) had her office on the same floor of Arts Block –I where we had our English Department. I talked to her. She was more than happy to be with us one afternoon....

She brought a rudimentary tape recorder with her,

a novelty in those years as a teaching aid that she used for her students of spoken French. The baby's parents and I sat on chairs a little distance away while Mrs. Bool Chand sat next to her on the bed. Suddenly the baby started speaking, beseechingly, urgently. Mrs. Bool Chand switched on the recorder. Once or twice she interjected and asked a short question in French, to which the baby replied after a moment's hesitation. It was indeed an awe-inspiring moment for all of us. Then suddenly the baby woke up and started crying. She wouldn't be pacified till her mother took her into the other room.

"I don't fully know," said Mrs. Bool Chand, "but her babyish speech was clear. She wanted her mom who had been taken forcibly away by soldiers ...." And then, being the senior-most in age, she advised, "Don't go to physicians or psychiatrists ... Let me find someone for you who can read more in her words than I can."

A few days later she came with an elderly gentleman and told us that he was a friend from Pondicherry, a French enclave in India where French was still included in school curriculum. The man was Franco-Indian, with a French father and an Indian mother. The specialty about him was that he was steeped in Indian devotional lore as, after his parents had died in an accident, he was brought up in the Krishnamurthy ashram. He stayed with my friend and his family for three days, befriended the little baby, sat with her during daytime and slept next to her crib in a rocking chair. He spoke to her in the particular jargon of French while she slept peacefully, but occasionally she answered his questions in a voice that was still babyish but a little different from her own.

His final diagnoses were that the baby was re-born to this young couple in this, the latest of her birth-cycles. Her story went back almost thirty years, in the waning years of World War II, when she was born, a French baby in and her mother was herded with other young French women in a truck by Nazi soldiers. She was left crying in her crib where she died soon after. She had had three more births but each time she died in infancy. This was her fourth incarnation and she was still searching for her original mother...

The old man's face got more wrinkled, he said, "I am sorry, I don't know but she might survive this time. She has a loving mom and a loving dad and she is free of her bonds to Europe."

I lost touch with my young friend when he went back to Montreal a few months later. However, back in 1982, while visiting friends in Toronto, I found an old diary with his phone number and called him. He was overjoyed and asked me to come over to Ottawa where he was teaching. I took a coach and reached Ottawa where he was waiting for me at the bus stand. We went, first to the City College where he was the Chairman of the Faculty and then to his house. I never asked him about his wife and daughter. However, when we got out of his car and he went ahead to open his locked house, he just said: "You do want to know, don't you?" And when I nodded, he said, "Soon after we repaired to Montreal, Jenny died before her fourth birthday."

"What about your wife?" I never asked this question, but while having a drink inside his small, sparsely furnished house, he said, "Joan couldn't bear the loss. Somehow, somewhere, I don't know how and why, she had cultivated this belief that if we had another child, it would be the same girl and she would die again….. So, we decided to plow the lonely furrows of our lives alone."

My friend, (I have never revealed his name for obvious reasons) is now no more. We have been in touch during these years. He expired three years ago of kidney failure. About Joan, his wife, I had no idea then or now. Whether the little girl's soul has found her real mother or is still searching for her hopping from one human body to another, I really don't know-.

$$* \quad * \quad *$$

A Spiritual Regression Session

It was during my short stay (1982) on the campus of British Columbia University, Vancouver, Canada that I heard from a faculty member that in the nearby Washington State that there was a Buddhist *ashram* (monastery) with a distinct program that many had attended. The monastery and its school were run by an American lady who had embraced Buddhism while she was in Nepal and chose to be renamed Renuka Devi Saraswati. The program, I was told, was called "Spiritual Regression" and volunteer subjects had to sign a contract of sorts absolving the *ashram* of any responsibility in case the subject suffered some kind of mental damage during the session.

I chose to go with an old Irish lady colleague who thought she would also volunteer for the session. There was no cash fee. The only condition was that the recordings done during the *session* as also the account of what happened to the subjects narrated by them after the session and recorded by the priestess were the copyright property of the *ashram* and could not be printed or shared with public or press.

My colleague, the Catholic lady from Ireland was senior to me by about twenty years and she opted to be the first *examinee*. It took her about two hours to be closeted inside a room with the Buddhist lady. I had filled in my contract form by the time she came out and offered to go inside as there were no others waiting for their turn. However, for reasons unknown I was rejected as a *candidate* but asked to come after a month or so when I was in a "better state of mind". I dare not argue and ask what my state of mind was and how it could not endure the session on that particular day. So I meekly accepted the preposition.

It is a different story that I never had the time or choice or inclination to go back after a month. However, my conversation with my colleague, Professor Mary Wright (the name is fictional) brought quite a few points that I pondered over for weeks. There was no clause in the contract that a 'subject' could not share his experiences with others. What she told me I reproduce here, not verbatim, but whatever I remember.

"I am seventy-two now, Dr. Anand," she said, "someone who has seen the world around, has a husband, three grown up kids and an academic career about to conclude. I had all but forgotten about some instances in my life that I thought were just dreams or bad memories and had never occurred in actuality..."

"...The session began with me lying down on a canopied bed while the Buddhist lady chanted her *mantras* – not the same mantra, but different ones. I was told to close my eyes and think of white clouds in the sky. I don't know how much time I took to slip into obvious oblivion but her voice was suggestive. 'You are now twenty ... go back ... you are now fifteen ...'"

"...At that point, as it happened, the clock struck and I started speaking. I could hear myself in a dreamy sort of a way. .."

"... I seem to be telling my story to no one in particular. When I was fifteen, I said, I was raped by an uncle of sorts, not a sugar daddy, mind you, but someone who was a father-figure in our family. I became pregnant. I was in the third month of pregnancy and lest people start noticing and I tell my family about the culprit 'uncle', he took me to a midwife of sorts who performed the illegal procedure of abortion.. I had the termination of my pregnancy. I was told that the fetus was feminine and was destroyed with other medical waste in the electric hearth...."

"...It was indeed a traumatic experience. My innards healed very soon but I had wild dreams. Invariably in these dreams the doll-like face of a little girl cried and accused me of killing her. 'You had no right to kill me,' it said in its babyish tone. Night after night, I broke out in cold sweat and, even with the help of a sleeping pill, I could not sleep after this vivid dream that I had a dozen or more times… Later, its frequency of occurrence decreased, and finally, it stopped altogether…"

"Did you tell your story the way you are narrating to me now, I mean, in the past tense and in the form of a narrative … like a story, I mean?" I asked.

"… No, I was probably speaking like a running commentator. As if the things were happening to me *here and now* and not *there and then*…"

I nodded my head. I knew about the *séances* with the holy men in India and how they mesmerized the subjects to deep sleep. I nodded my head again. "Please go on …"

She continued. "During my *session here* all this came back to me … yes, came back to me with a vengeance. There always was this little girl, with her accusing little finger pointed at me, but she never told me about what happened after she had been k*illed* by me. In this session she had a laughing face. She told me that she was the winner after all. She had come back to me and passed through the same birth channel that was denied to her before … for, she said, that had been her destiny for countless birth cycles. She *had* to be my daughter …I had never had this part of the revelation in my dream sequences as a girl, but now I *know* that she came back to me as a baby in flesh."

"…When I had my first delivery, it was a girl. I was sure that she **was** the reincarnation of the soul I had so mercilessly denied a place in my womb. I treated her as a special baby. Even my friends noticed that I was extraordinarily attached to her. But there was no visible sign from her side. Three years later I had another baby, a girl again….And then, two years later, I had another baby. This time also it was a girl…"

The only question I could ask her was about any guess as to which one of her three children, she thought, was really the original soul.

It was a sad smile she gave me. "How would I know which one of these three is my *blessed* or *accursed* daughter that I had killed before she was born? They are all alike. There is no distinguishing mark anywhere. I always hoped that I would get a sign in a dream, but now I do not have a recurrence of those dreams."

*   *   *

GOLD TREASURE IN MY NATIVE VILLAGE

It was after a lapse of 57 years that I returned to my ancestral village, Kot Sarang, in Pakistan. In 1947, Hindus were turned out from their centuries old abodes or left of their own accord from the newly created nation when it was carved out of the ancient land of India. Kot Sarang is a nondescript village in the Northeastern Gandhara cultural belt of Punjab. As history tells us, before the advent of Buddhism and the mushrooming forth of Buddhist reliquaries, sanctums and monuments, this area marked by stunted hillocks and shallow valleys could boast of a Shiva worship zone. Shiva worship subsided during the Buddhist heyday but was refurbished, alongside Islamic Sufi shrines by the rise of the Yogi cult in 14th and 15th century Punjab. As it is, *yogis* lived an ascetic life, full of hard *yogic samadhi* practice sessions, ate frugally and went about the town, exactly like Buddhist *bhikshu* mendicants, begging uncooked food. They were forbidden to take money, apparel, ornaments or ostentatious gifts.

The wandering ascetics, all disciples of Guru Gorakh Nath, founded small sanctuaries as Shiva temples in this area with attached schools of *yogic* practice for new entrants called *baawas* or *oghars* before they became full-fledged *yogis*. Their hall-mark was a pair of perforated ears with dangling rings, thick and hard, called *mundras*. With the Islamic culture intermingling with Hindu culture, a *yogic* sanctuary was called *durgah* which, in fact, is an appellation for a Muslim holy shrine or place of gathering for the devout. One such *durgah* was founded in the rein of Maharaja Ranjit Singh in Kot Sarang, my ancestral village. Hindu children born in the village were baptized by the Head of the sanctuary designated as *Peer* which also is a Muslim title for a religious leader. I was sixteen years of age when I left Pakistan in 1947. I was one of a chosen few whom Peer Ram Nath, the Head of the *durgah* at Kot Sarang held very dear because while studying in Nowshehra and Rawalpindi I had gathered a rich knowledge of religious sects in Hinduism, the Gorakh Nath cult being one of them and could discuss matters, material and spiritual, with him at an equal level.

With their men folk mostly having been killed at the time of the partition of the country, Peer Ram Nath had herded hapless women and children inside the sanctuary of the *durgah* and was trying to arrange for a bus (called *lorry*) to transport them to the Refugee camps in Rawalpindi. To the women he gave a few gold coins from the underground treasure-trove of the *durgah*, so they should carry it hidden in their clothes to India to start a new life. My mother was one such lady who was given five gold coins of the East India Company era.

The presence of an underground treasure, buried inside the four walls of the *durgah* was a common knowledge and, back in 1919, my own grandfather Lala Buta Mal was gunned down by a group of Afghan dacoits who had come to rob the sanctuary of its gold but, since the *Peer Sahib* was away, they could not get its location from any one of the other inmates. In the process they had gunned down some villagers. These included my grandfather also.

This background was necessary for me before recounting the para-normal experience I got when I went to visit Kot Sarang half a century after having left the place of my birth.

For a day that I stayed in my village, my local host was Ali Mohammad Farshi, a well-known Urdu poet and a fast friend. He was married to the daughter of a prominent person of the village who took me around the village streets, landmarks, old sites, scenes and spots. While it would have been a soulful experience to see the old *durgah's* sprawling building, my heart missed a beat or two when I found that was not there. It had been demolished during 1947 and the looters had decamped with not only the large stock of food grain, the live stock, but also the building material. A few houses had come up on the level ground where the children played *kabbaddi* or *football*. At one spot, my host halted and told me, "This, Dr. Anand, is the place where the cemented platform held aloft the *Shiva*-flag of the *durgah* on a steel pole. The steel pole and the flag were removed by the looters, the cemented platform was dug up but the hard rock beneath still shows it as a conspicuous point, jutting out from the surrounding level ground."

I stood there for a few minutes. Lost in reverie, I thought of the time when I saw this flag fluttering in the wind.......And then, *suddenly* I had the uncanny experience of walking, as if in a haze, a narrow but short underground tunnel and finally stopping and standing in front of a golden door.

Short, dwarfed as it were to a three-foot high size, it was half open. Inside the small cave-like rock pit, was a steel box. This *sandooq,* as it was called in the local lingua, was brimming with shining gold coins. There would have been a few hundred, if not a few thousand *mohrs* in it. I stood transfixed. Petrified, with my feet heavy with fatigue and my head bent in the low-ceiling tunnel, I could breathe with difficulty. The scene, however, was so real that I felt a hidden desire to step into the inner sanctum of wealth and feel the coins with my own hands. Well, something inside me told me to halt, go back to my own world and dare not disturb this universe frozen in time.

It must have taken me well nigh ten to fifteen minutes in tracing the path back from this cavern through the dark tunnel under the rock, because suddenly I found my host holding me by my hand and saying, "Come on, Professor Sahib, let's now go back. There is no fun standing here and dreaming about the past with your eyes shut.

Was it a reverie? Indeed, was it a daydream of fantastic proportions? Was it a heightened, feverish state of mind creating a sudden protrusion of something that had remained hidden for years? Indeed, was it a revelation of something really hidden, buried under my feet, that my mind could authenticate. ...

On being prompted by my host, I woke up, as if from a reverie. Shuddering inside, but not showing any outward sign of what I had experienced, I did not talk about this uncanny day-dream, simply because I knew treasure seekers would dig up the entire ground in search of the gold coins.

I declined to stay for the night at the residence of Ali Mohammad Farshi's in-law's house, for I was not sure if I would have a series of nightmares at night. Before returning the same evening by car to Rawalpindi, I said a final good-bye to my home, the streets of Kot Sarang and the centuries' old soil of the village in which were mixed the ashes of a dozen or more generations of my ancestors. I prayed that I should, at that moment of departure, be set free permanently of the shackles of my fond and foolish memories. I would never ever come back again.

Then, almost eleven years later, in the early months of 2014, when I went to Rawalpindi again, I was driven by the Chairman of the Academy of Letters and my valued friend Mr. Abdul Hameed – to Talagang, the Tehsil headquarters of Kot Sarang and a mere ten kilometers from my birthplace. Talagang was my maternal grandfather's home town and I wanted to see the house wherein I had played with my maternal cousins. He asked me if I would like to visit the village of my birth … and, without a moment's hesitation, I said, "No, Sir."

While we were in Talagng, local friends who had gathered there for a courtesy meeting asked me twice why I did not want to go to my birth place. I dreaded the question, but then I simply told them that I was dead tired and would like to go back to Rawalpindi.

* * *

THE ZEN BORDERLAND OF MIND

The story of my experimentation with Buddhism

It is important for me to add some excerpts from my book ONE HUNDRED BUDDHAS (Trafford 2011), for readers to place this section of the book in its proper prospective.

THE FIRST DISCIPLE OF BUDDHA

(1)   Who *was* Anand? Who *is* Anand?

A personal note

Before I begin this preamble, let me answer both questions in one sentence. The first Anand was Buddha's chosen disciple twenty-six centuries back; the second Anand is the present writer who claims to be the first Anand's nava-sarupa. *(The Reincarnated-self).*

I was born in a nondescript village situated in the Gandhara cultural belt of present day Punjab in Pakistan in 1931. In pre-Islamic and post-Brahmanic period (3rd century B.C. to 5th century A.D.) this tract of land was dotted with Buddhist viharas and schools for bhikshus. One of the two Buddhist universities in India was located at Takshila (now Taxla) on the banks of the river Indus in present day Pakistan. It attracted students not only from India but from adjoining countries as well. I was christened in the Hindu way as Satyapal but my clan name was 'Anand'. I was curious and I researched the origin of my clan or tribe right from my high school days.

I was surprised to learn from an old cousin of my deceased grandpa that Anands were a tribe founded by a Buddhist bhikshu of that name. He told me that the bhikshu Anand was on his way to Afghanistan with five others who also had the same names with different add-ons. While Anand, the leader of the group of five used only one name, the other four were: Anand Sarthi, Anand Sakhshi, Anand Shauri and Anand Shramiki. They stayed as guests of the local chieftain of a tribe called Khokhar, a tribe settled on both sides of the river Indus. Two days after their arrival, the young virgin daughter of the chieftain went to bhikshu Anand where he was doing his mantra-path after a dip in the river and bedecked him with a garland made of lotus flowers. This was a declarative symbol that she had chosen him as her husband.

Lala Beli Ram, my paternal grandfather's cousin, could not give me many details but he had heard the story from his father and grandfather, and they from their fathers and grandfathers, and so on before him. He was sure of its authenticity. Anand, the bhikshu on his way to Gandhara (Kandahar in Afghanistan) is reported to have given up his ascetic life as a bhikshu, got married to the girl and settled down with a lease of land from his bride's father. So did his four compatriots who married other girls of the clan and all chose to settle down as tillers and traders. Thus a new sub-clan came into being. It was called "Anand". It continued to retain its original links to the Khokhar tribe.

As a young man I vowed to find my lineage and whether or not I was, in some way, related to the original Anand. This being a common name all over India and South East Asia, it was well nigh a wild guess, but I felt it was in my blood to know who Anand the bhikshu who had married the chieftain's daughter really was.

It was only after my appointment as a lecturer of English in the Punjab University, Chandigarh that I took up the study once again. Sanskrit and Hindi I already knew but I learnt a bit of Pali language and started reading whatever I could find on the period. I was encouraged by Pundit Hazari Prasad Diwedi who had come over to our university as Head of the Hindi Department. He got me a few books from Varanasi also. It was, however, a chance meeting with a scholar from Kurukshetra University that let me jump into the deep caverns of written history, folk tales, and what not. Dr. Buddha Prakash of Kurukshetra University was an authority on Punjab castes, clans and tribes, and he confirmed the origin of the Anand sub-clan of Khokhars. After the advent of Islam in India through the bad lands of Afghanistan and conversions of Hindus to that faith, those of the clan who became Muslims retained their original clan name Khokhar but those who continued to be Hindus called themselves a little differently, viz. Khokharain.

Khokhars were known to have inhabited the tract of land on both sides of the river Indus from times immemorial. There is a mention of the Raja Paurushva being a Khokhar king, (popularly known as Pauras who fought the last battle against the invading forces of Alexander, the Great,—356-323 B.C), there was no way of knowing when (particularly in what century) the five bhikshus had arrived there and then gave up their chosen faith to become tillers and farmers. Buddha, (Siddhartha-Gautama) lived in 563?-482? B.C., that is more than 2 centuries before Alexander's invasion of India, and since Anand, the first disciple of Buddha was his contemporary, there was no way of the bhikshu who became a member of the Khokharain clan being the original Anand. It can be surmised, however, that the name being a common nomenclature for individuals and clans all over India, a branch of the Buddhist bhikshus also ran a clan of that name and the one who settled down in that area was just the patrol leader of the group of five bhikshus, and that he had nothing to do with the original Anand, the chosen disciple of Buddha.

So, my final discovery was that over twenty or more centuries my original lineage has been attached to one of the five monks who chose to become khokhars. This is the one and only reason for my attachment with Buddhism. For years during this formative period I would often dream about monks going from door to door, myself being a part of the group of four or five.

One thing that I noticed in particular was that during these dream sequences I never had the good fortune to "see" Buddha himself. Was this an ordained part of my destiny that I would write poems in Urdu, English and Hindi about Buddhism? Well, I don't know, but I have done it—and this might be my remission now that I am eighty years old and cannot look forward to many years of active work.

* * *

A SHUDDERING EXPERIENCE

Introductory Note

There are no authentic details of Bhikshu Anand's original tribe or village or how he came over and became the most trusted disciple of Buddha, nor was there any mention of where he went after Buddha's demise, what he did, and how he died.

Cunningham, the historian, has mentioned that Anand was the only male issue of a rich family in Sanchi, a town near the Nepal border. He heard Buddha speak to a crowd of people and followed him to the next and then to the next village. Thus he became, not exactly the first, but one of the first few of Buddha's followers, and, finally, at the time of the founding of the institution called Buddha Viharas or Ashrams; he looked after the welfare of the inmates to let Buddha himself have enough time for his samadhi samagams. Eugene Burnouf, in his *A History of Indian Buddhism, (1844),* has enumerated Anand's numerous birth spans prior to the one as Buddha's disciple. He has used the material available in Jataka Stories, that, many believe to be a work of fiction that does not give any factual history.

The Royal Asiatic Society of London rejected Cunningham's account of the birth and spread of Buddhism and sent Markham Kittoe, a historian by discipline, to India to travel to the area originally chosen by Buddha for the propagation of his beliefs, collect whatever material he can by way of folk tales, old manuscripts or inscriptive writings on rocks. "The Chinese travelers in fifteenth and sixteenth centuries, or even earlier, had already collected a fairly large haul of this material and there was hardly anything left."

Kittoe presented two reports to the Royal Asiatic Society but only one of these two was published. The other was left to be opened after his death. It was this report that somehow was stolen and then surfaced in Sri Lanka, then known as Ceylon. It is in this report that Kittoe gives a graphic account of his search for the place where Anand was supposed to have been attacked by the demon Marra. After reading the report I thought that I myself would like to go and visit the Tarai countryside in search of the famed Gridh Kitta.

In 1964, during summer vacations in the university I under took a two days rail journey from Delhi. It wasn't difficult for me to find my destination. Many a tourist goes to Bodhgaya and now there are quite a few stores selling hand-made and machine-made small Buddha icons. Taxies take the tourists to the point in the Rajgir valley where a steep path climbs up like serpent to the top of the Vultures' Peak. Like many others I also walked to the mound. "There it was," I wrote in my diary, "the mound known till today as *Gridh kitta*. 'Gridh' means a vulture in Hindi 'kitta' is just a mound. I was quite young and given to walking long tracts of land, but climbing was a task in itself. It took me a hour or so, and by the time I reached the top, my water bottle was empty.

The top was like a table top with a small brick-laid enclosure. I didn't know who had built it but it looked modern because the bricks were baked. It took me a few minutes to catch my breath, as the sight of the valley was so absorbing that I could not detach my eyes from it.

With my eyes closed I sat there for at least two hours. I had reveries of the kind I cannot explain. To me some times it seemed as if I was a vulture myself sitting on top of the mound and scanning the countryside around for some small animals as my prey. Occasionally I felt like I was watching the nearby cave with its mouth now squarely covered by forest growth. What was inside—was a question that my vulture mind asked again and again." Then again I felt as if I was inside the cave, sitting cross-legged with my eyes closed but an uncanny sight-restoring moment, even with closed eyes, I had the glimpse of a vulture looking at me with its beady eyes.   I must have shuddered but I woke up from this 'daydream'. I had a cold sweat. It took me well nigh half an hour to get ready for my descent from the peak.

I stayed overnight in a pilgrim's *dhramshala*. The next day, very early in the morning I went to the mound again. The record in my diary reads like this.

"I stood upright on Gridh Kitta for a long time. Suddenly I felt a sudden body heat as if I was on fire, the fire leaping from my body and turning me into a human torch. I had the notion that with the fire engulfing my body, I was supposed to fly and enter the cave where a young *tapassavi* has to be burnt alive . . . A few minutes later the reverie passed and I was myself again."

This strange experience could have been my own imagination, but, of course, it is somehow related to the third attack by the demon Marra in which he sets himself on fire and flies into the cave to end Anand's life in a fiery death.

Three things have now come to my mind while writing this account. One is Lord Buddha's own account of his encounter with Mara, the demon, himself and then with his messengers of death, his two daughters, whom the demon had sent one after the other, to beguile and thus put an end to Buddha's penance. I have written all three of Buddha's encounter with the demon and his tribe in *One Hundred Buddhas* and I am reproducing it here.

The second is my own account that I am presenting as an excerpt from the 'End Notes' of *One Hundred Buddhas*. It seems important to me to expostulate it fully for readers who do not have any grounding in Indian culture or those who have not read my book and the auxiliary notes on some portions of it.

The third is a chance discovery of an account of Dalai Lama's visiting the *Gridh Kitta*, (Vultures' Peak) and (lest I am accused of infringing the copy right of the book) I am reproducing it in the form of short quotations. The bibliographical particulars of the book are as under: His Holiness Dalai Lama and Victor Chan, *the Wisdom of Forgiveness* (New York: Riverbead Books: 2004).

EXTRACT – 1.

(One Hundred Buddhas)

THE DEMON MARRA

And then it so happened.

"I have been trying to ask you for many days, O' Master But couldn't find the courage . . . .

Well, today, I have . . . I have . . .

Who was the demon Marra, O' Swami?"

He abruptly asked.

The Master looked at him quizzically, but kept quiet.

"O' Master, is my question improper?"

This time Buddha spoke.

His tone was firm, his words clear and measured but pointed.

"Don't you yourself remember Marra the demon, O' Anand? You also had a brush with him."

Anand was rather taken aback.

"Oh, No, Master, I never had anything to do with him.

Who was he?"

"You called him a demon.

And you also called him by his name Marra.

So, it seems you know him or at least something about him. You have known him, my disciple. Don't you?"

Anand was just flabbergasted.

"No, I don't O' Tathagata,

The name Marra just surfaced in my mind.
Again and again it came with the image of a vulture.
So I thought I would ask you."
"So, partially you remember, O' Anand.
Marra it was who tried to dissuade you from meditation. Marra it
was who came and swooped over you as a vulture.
You just woke up but he couldn't harm you
As you didn't raise a hand to defend yourself."
Anand was deep in thought trying to remember something.
The Lord said
"O' Anand, Gridh Kitta was the mound
Do you remember the name?"
"Yes, O' Master, I do.
The mound and the nearby cave I know.
Inside that cave I sat for my samadhi, and
. . . and . . . I now remember . . .
A vulture came many times
It shrieked obscenities at me.
It struck its wings against the cave side
Finally, O' Master, having opened just one eye
when I didn't pay attention
and went back into deep meditation
it flew away."
. "That was Marra, the demon, O' Anand.
The evil forces had sent him to interrupt your *samadhi*.
You were not disturbed for you were strong.
Strong in your resolve and your meditative depth.
I wish you had been a little stronger . . ."
"A little stronger, O' my Guru?
I was strong but I could have been stronger, how?"
"Had you been stronger, O' Anand
Your opened eye would have struck like lightening
I don't know if it could have killed him
but he would have been rendered harmless.
He then couldn't have done any more mischief."
The Lord paused for a while, and then said again.

"To dissuade me from my path
Marra didn't come himself.
He was afraid that I would obliterate him
if I ever opened my eyes.
So he sent his daughters, one after another
Two of them . . .
He didn't come himself to disturb my Samadhi."
"O' Master," said Anand eagerly.
"Please do tell me about what happened.
Did you obliterate his two daughters?"
"No, I didn't—for I don't kill.
At least I don't kill women even if they're demons.
So I rendered them barren."
"Some other day, O' Anand," the master continued.
"Some other day
I would tell you about Marra's daughters.
Worth telling it would be
Worth getting rid of these memories."
                    (Anand: ***One Hundred Buddhas***. Pp.103-09)

                    *   *   *

Extract – 2

(One Hundred Buddhas)

MARRA'S ELDER DAUGHTER

Buddha spoke to Anand.
"This account of what happened to me,
O' Anand, is engraved in my alter-memory.
I don't know how much of this actually happened
and how much of it my memory has just made up.
But listen, O' *Jigyasu!*"
"I fasted for many lunar months, O' Anand.
The bow tree I had chosen was an old one;
like a cloak it screened me from sun and rain.
Curtained, covered, protected—once I sat
With no asana under my bare lower self
I didn't know what was happening around."
…Sometimes the tree
like a mother to her baby talked to me;
it told me the news of weather, wind and sun.
Most of the time, I just stayed sunk in my essential *buddhi*
maybe, deeper than anyone had gone before I don't know. I
uncovered layers upon layers of darkness—
and then one day . . . ."
The pause was longer than usual.
So Anand blurted out,

"Yes. O' Master, then what happened?"
Buddha said, "I was about to uncover the last layer …
see the light shining underneath and fill my spirit with it,
but . . . . . . but suddenly I found the external world impinging on
me. There was a sound, sweeter than paradisiacal harmony.
Ecstatic bliss it was—
that human sound, a female voice.
It said:
I am here O' Gautama; I have come to meet you."
Once again, Anand was almost on pins and needles.
When the pause became longer, he asked, "So, O' My Guru?"
Buddha continued, "It wasn't the voice alone
it was also the scent of her body
—and more so of her hair.
My Yashodha, it seemed, had come to meet me.
I refrained from opening my eyes
but it seemed the voice and the scent
was enveloping me like a warm blanket.
There seemed no way out
either to accept or to challenge.
I chose the latter."
Anand spoke almost instantaneously
"You challenged the woman, O' Master?
"Did she tell you, who she was, O' Master?"
"Yes, she did.
She fell at my feet and begged me to forgive her.
She told me she was Marra's elder daughter.
'Don't burn me, O ascetic," she said
"I am just eighteen years old
not even married.
I will do no evil in future.'"
"So, O' Tathagata, you let her be?"
"If I had blasted her with one angry glance
I would have last half of my spiritual gain.
So, I compromised.
I turned her barren for all her life.

No off-spring, no sons or daughters, no more evil.
And I did it with her concurrence.
I told her that either it was death or this.
She agreed . . .
and I was saved of losing my spiritual gain."
"O' my clever Master!" said Anand.

(Anand: *One Hundred Buddhas:* Pp 111-15)

*   *   *

MY MEETINGS WITH THE DALAI LAMA

FIRST MEETING

As the youngest faculty member in the Department of English, Panjab University, Chandigarh, I had the privilege of keeping the company of my students almost at an equal level. Problems, personal and emotional, that they dare not take to older teachers, they would bring to me to get my advice and, like a true *confidante,* I would keep their trust.

One by-product of this was the weekend excursions that some of us, (I at the head of a group of six to ten students), both boys and girls, took to the nearby Shivalik hills. At least once every year I would take a group to Dharamsala, a hill resort in the lower Himalayas, where we stayed at dak bungalows and wandered about, taking pictures and meeting hill people.

A definite attraction was the presence of a large number of Tibetans, both monks and ordinary folk, who had come down in the wake of Chinese occupation of this Buddhist nation. Dalai Lama, the Head of the religious order as also of the autonomous region of Tibet recognized both by the British and the Chinese from 19th century onwards, was there. Not always because he had his international visits, but we would enquire about his travel itinerary before we left for the hill station so that we could have his *darshan also.*

It was a sunny morning in this town while, it seemed, the fog had rolled down into the valleys and gorges when we all went to the public enclosure where the grand *guru* came to greet his visitors. I was one of a hundred nondescript men and women of all ages. There was nothing to distinguish me from others – and yet, what electrified me was the fact that Dalai Lama, surrounded by two of his aids, came down the three stairs of the wide verandah – and walked straight to me.

Inwardly I trembled with – what? Apprehension? Foreboding fear? Was it love or reverence? I just didn't know, but when stopped in front of me, my head automatically bowed, I tried to touch his feet. He bid me not to do it, then looked deep into my eyes and said in English, "Anand ...It took you so long to come to your compatriot."

I wasn't taken aback; just let the question sink into my whole being before I said, "Yes, your holiness, it took me so long for there is always a time and place for special events." .... I really don't know what made me utter this seemingly philosophical but otherwise a very ordinary saying so common in speech, but he smiled .....

Yes, he smiled, put both his hands on my shoulders and said, "Try to get to know yourself, Anand, who once waited at his Master's bidding and then, in each succeeding cycle, tried hard but could not reach him."

He traced a step back and went about his routine of greeting people. Before he did so, one of the two monks with him handed me a small replica of the fasting Buddha and said, "You've been blessed. Go and do your work. Your name and fame both are blessed now."

My students who had accompanied me were in great awe and asked me many questions to which I had but just one answer. "Anand," I said, "is the magical word that triggered off the sequence." "But how did he know your name, Sir?" They asked almost in unison. "I don't know," I said, "except that. ... Anand was the name of Lord Buddha's first disciple and his *confidante*. ..

But I knew that I *knew*

And later one of them told me that she knew that I *knew*.

*   *   *

SECOND MEETING

Preamble

I had taken my pre-retirement leave for six months and was preparing to follow my family to USA when I got a letter from Dharamshala, the Dalai Lama's abode in India. It was unsigned, just a printed circular about the forthcoming Tenth Mind and Life Conference. A phone number had been given and I forthwith made a call. It took a while for the Indian-Tibetan voice to understand what I wanted to know about the Conference.

My simple question was – "Am I invited?" Then after a couple of minutes, a male voice came on the line that spoke clear English, "I am Thupten Jimpa, Dr. Anand. I am the English interpreter of His Holiness."

"Yes, "I said, "Yes, Sir, Have I been invited?"

Pat came the answer, "Yes, Dr. Anand. Your name *is* on the list of invitees. It took us some time to know your present address. The original letter was sent to your address on our Visitors' Register that you signed in 1965 when you came here. This letter bounced from Chandigarh. So we sent this letter at your Department of English address. You have probably moved from your house to another location."

The proper invitation letter soon came. I had not been invited as a speaker or a participant but as an attendee. I sent my consent letter, told my wife and children in USA that my visit would be delayed and waited for the day – almost with bated breath. Something of a miracle in itself was the fact that mine would be one of the thousands of names on the visitors' register and that it had been tick-marked (by whom?)....

Dharamshala

I went to Dharamshala, registered my name in the Reception Office; I was given a room in the *galleria* – just two rooms removed from Steven Chu, the American Nobel laureate in physics. A loner, probably in his real life, I couldn't even get a responding smile from him, much less a handshake, but when I said while passing and stopping by him in the corridor, "I have always hated mathematics", he looked at me, a flickering smile came and was gone in no time, "Math is hard to cultivate friendship with .." And he turned away without waiting for a response from me. Victor Chan was more forthcoming. He earned his fame later when he co-authored the book *the Wisdom of Forgiveness* with the Dalai Lama. However, at that time he was but one delegate among many. However, his physical proximity with His Holiness was marked by all of us because of his presence, everywhere, alongside the Dalai Lama. The other constant companion, understandably, was Thupten Jimpa, the English interpreter who had talked to me on phone.

I got permission from the private office of the Dalai Lama to be with the delegates. About sixty they were, mostly men, some attendees like me, half a dozen invited guests, some Tibetan monks – all jostling for space in the rather dingy hall inside the Dalai Lama's residential compound. First day's topic was "The Nature of Matter: The Nature of Life", The presenters for the five-day colloquium were a galaxy of genomic research scholars, evolutionary biology experts from India, Japan, Sri Lanka, USA and U.K. Buddhist experts were a category apart. A group of three, all neurologists from the West moved around showing a sense of intimate camaraderie with all.

When His Holiness entered, I noticed two things at once. I had first seen him in 1963 and now it was almost a quarter century hence. He had changed physically. Then he looked fresh and young. Now the age seemed to be creeping on him in diverse ways. Like many Tibetan monks he had rounded shoulders that scooted forward to give the appearance of a hunch. I had read somewhere that a man in that posture displays a subconscious body language intimating humility. With the Dalai Lama, this pronounced stoop had become an ossified permanent mark of *selflessness*. It seemed to say, "Body, the unimportant part of *self* ages, decays, dies: Spirit the most important part of *self* gains, shines, becomes beautiful in proportion to this decay of the body."

Now follows a set of notes from my diary of the period.

Dalai Lama said: "I meditate the simplest way. I conjure up visual images of people in general around me and reach out to them... I transfer my positive visualizations of love, gratitude, affection, happiness. They hold their hands out and I clasp them warmly in my own hands..."

Dalai Lama said, "A set of other visualizations emerges. There are people who suffer enormously: Physical pain, grief over loss of a dear one, sorrow, a feeling of emptiness, a vacuum, as it were in life. I share it with them. Often times I take it all ... I feel their misery myself, but it passes, like an electric current from head to foot and vanishes in the earth below my feet. I breathe it in myself and ... then breathe it out. Their suffering is gone while I suffer but only for one moment..."

Dalai Lama said, "Lest they feel empty, I replace fresh air, aroma of flowers and incense burning and thus fill up the vacuum created by loss of painful feelings ... I call it 'giving and taking' ..."

Dalai Lama said, "This, in short, is the way I meditate. I do not lose myself in a vacuumated sphere of nothingness. I am always with people, with life – and with myself."

The first set of Notes in my diary ends here.

* * *

Faith and Science

While walking out for our lunch, I approached Victor Chen and begged him to let me sit for a while with him and His Holiness as I was keen to renew the special relationship that I had with him. His quizzical look made me answer in a bland way. "His Holiness recognized me several years ago as Anand in one of his life cycles." I half-dreaded that he would snicker in derision or just walk away from me, but he stopped in his tracks, looked at me again – and yet again – and then bowed before me. "Yes, Mr. Anand, I will see to it," he said, still bowing, to which was added a pair of folded hands.

The afternoon session was a memorable one. My pocket recorder had two tapes and it had the uncanny provision of automatic transference from one to the other if the first one was full. I just kept it on. I thought nobody noticed but there was a flicker of smile at the interpreter, Thupten Jimpa's lips. He knew – and I knew that he knew.

Steve Chu was the main speaker in this session. This physicist of Chinese origin had won the Nobel Prize in 1997. He specialization was laser light and his findings had revolutionized the concept, particularly in its actual application in medicine and surgery. His sense of humor, even during the dry-as-dust concepts, kept the audience laughing. Then came the real moments when His Holiness spoke.

*   *   *

My diary records the exact words of His Holiness as interpreted in English by Thupten Jimpa.

"The dialogue between scientists and Buddhist can broaden the horizon of knowledge. In our schools for the Tibetan monks, we have prescribed essential scientific studies ...All of the humanity wants happiness. It is a universal goal of each human being. Development of inner self is essential to achieve this. Emotions, I am talking about. I am off the subject of heaven, liberation from the birth cycle and the like, just pure, simple, unalloyed happiness. Promotion of human values, a sense of caring and sharing – these are values of individual conduct. Herein is the secret of *inner self* modulating the *outer self.* I would go a step further and say the *vice verse* is also right. It is in this that the scientists can help. Yet neither they, nor religious men like me, can take precedence over each other."

(Notes in my diary conclude here).

There was a fifteen minutes' recess for Tibetan tea. I kept on jostling with others to be as much near in proximity to the Dalai Lama as I could. And then, suddenly he turned to me, and said with an unmistaken sense of – What was it? Humor…Was it?

"There were no scientists then, Anand. Were there any?"

And without waiting for an answer, he turned away to talk to others.

*   *   *

THIRD MEETING

The third session of the day was indeed the most fruitful. For an uninitiated novice like me, a lot of points became clear. One reason was that the interpreter was now a monk, Tenzin Geyche, who spoke very slowly, weighing each word. He was a middle-aged monk with deep lines on his face going from nowhere to nowhere.

However, for me the highlight was an interview the Dalai Lama gave to

(Some notes from my diary, noted from my tape recorder, after pruning and editing do not make any grammatical sense, but I have let this text be as it was in my diary.)

"….The concept of impermanence, and also of emptiness …very powerful, very useful … Nagarjuna, the Indian thinker defines emptiness as interdependency or interconnectedness …"

My own comment: Nagarjuna was the 2nd Century A.D. Indian thinker whose writings became the basics of Tibetan Buddhism.

Notes in my diary continue …

"… Emptiness does not mean nothingness … Emptiness is full, not empty. The realization of intellectual understanding …it is. We cal also consider it as interdependence … helps us widen our view. That is our view toward the world, our view toward our own life. It really widens our perspective. It is helpful in formulating this holistic view…"

*   *   *

EXTRACT – 3

Culled from *Wisdom of Forgiveness*

"Five Indian Commandos formed a human shield around the Dalai Lama as he trudged up the steep train leading to Vultures' Peak, one of the key pilgrimage sites for Buddhists. These soldiers, members of an elite unit in the Indian army, were dressed immaculately in black: long-sleeved cotton shirts, flowing head scarves, and crisply pressed pants.....More soldiers in khakis and blue berets, trailed behind. I had never seen Dalai Lama so well protected in India. It was a rare event for the Tibetan leader to be visiting this out-of-the-way pilgrimage site ......

The Dalai Lama climbed slowly but steadily, leaning with deliberation into a walking stick fashioned from a scrawny-looking branch. From time to time he chatted briefly with his Indian escorts, but mainly he kept to himself. A quarter of the way up, he took off the maroon outer shawl and handed it to Buchung, his attendant, who folded it carefully into a square packet. At one point, the Dalai Lama walked a few steps off the path to look at a small meditation cave dug into the side of the hill. A disciple of Buddha had cloistered himself there in meditation two and half millennia ago...."

(My own note: *This exactly was the cave I visualized during my 'shuddering experience" when, standing on top of the Vultures' Peak, in my reverie I felt the vulture about to pounce upon me).*

53

"By the time we reached the top of Vultures' Peak, the Dalai Lama was sweating. He stopped, reached inside his monk's tunic and pulled out a tissue, dabbing his forehead and face with it.... The top of the Vultures' Peak was handkerchief-sized piece of flat ground hemmed in by rocky outcrops on three sides. On the fourth, the knife-edged ridge dropped steeply down a valley. A U-shaped brick enclosure, built to waist height, dominated the flat area..."

(My own note: *Back in early Sixties of the last century, when I went alone, this brick enclosure was there but there were no candles.*

"After prostrations, the Dalai Lama walked to the edge of the ridge and looked down into the flat valley of Rajgir, three hours' drive from Bodhgaya....The view was gorgeous but Dalai Lama didn't linger over it. His mind was on the prayers – the wisdom sutras explaining the concept of emptiness – which he had come to recite."

*   *   *

CHRIST AS BUDDHA REBORN

I have already written in a previous shard about my visit to *Gridh Kitta* (The Vultures' Peak) and the reveries I experienced. It was much more than a mere series of reveries, I now recall as an after-thought when I let the succeeding flashes of these images emerge in my mind now. It is as if for all times to come these 'visuals' have dug their footprints deep in my mind. What indeed was in my subconscious mind has now surfaced and has become a part of my live memories. Experts in sub-retina studies of the eye claim that this phenomenon is called *mosaicism*. It is in the form of a mosaic image. It is that image produced by a compound eye in which each element *ommatidium* focuses and forms a very small part of the total view and cannot be remembered with all its visual content, but in dreams or waking reveries, one does achieve this faculty.

Yet another surprise waited for me when I talked to the villagers. Since I had picked up the rudimentary hybrid form of the local lingua, I talked to them with ease and understanding. It was in one such meeting with an elder in a village that I was suddenly asked question in this dialect: "Are you a Jesus?" I knew what he meant and I said, "No, I am a Hindu, not a Christian." "No!" He shook his head vehemently. "No!" he repeated. "What I meant was Jesus, the Tathagata! One that had to come after him …"

That opened a Pandora Box of local legends. In the centuries before this and the centuries after the demise of Lord Buddha, each wandering nomad, walking alone and trying to find remnants of Buddha's story was asked this question by the locals who believed in the next incarnation of Buddha. I extended my stay in the area by a week and talked to many, indeed, many other elders, mendicants, *sadhus,* soothsaying old women who told stories, all intermingled with Lord Krishna, Lord Buddha, Shiva and other Hindu gods. It was difficult to fathom the truth of these murky waters that ran in this stream of Buddha legend.

Finally, what emerged in my mind was a clear picture that at some time before his demise Buddha had proclaimed that the then live span that he had lived was not his last birth and that he had yet to get his *nirwana…* the last spoke in the cyclic wheel. For this, he would be born as a special messenger of the Holy Spirit and would be tortured and crucified. The word *Jisu* or *Eesu* or *Yisu,* in the local lingua means 'here', 'there' and 'all over', but it is also a name that people have revered for centuries. It seemed to me that in their collective subconscious there is a belief that the Master has to come back and that he would be known by this name.

That was the *rationabilins* of my poem that has already been included in my book *ONE HUNDRED BUDDHAS* published in 2011. It can be found as Extract-3 in this chapter.

Extract -4

JESUS CHRIST

(One Hundred Buddhas)

And then it so happened.
The crowd in the congregation dispersed
and even the last bhikshu, chanting his mantra
Buddham Sharnan Gachhami departed.
The Master was all by himself, alone
sitting cross-legged on his mat.
He was sunk in deep meditation.
He had told his disciples
that he would be busy for many days
visualizing his next life in the birth cycle
that a single span was the only one that remained
and he would achieve the nirvana
his release from the birth-death cyclic chain.
Anand, sitting next to him spoke in a low tone "O', the first among equals
O' my master in this and other lives
now grant me my wish to give up your companionship
as I also want to get my *nirvana*
after this life span is over."
Buddha spoke,
"Which *nirvana*, O Anand, my first disciple?

Which nirvana are you talking about?
Is it the same for which I
your master and mentor
have been tirelessly running from one birth to another? Changing
my paths evenly and alternately
O Anand, I have as yet not found my nirvana.
I have only reached the present link in my birth cycle
the link that you know as Buddha.
Come; speak up fearlessly
O' my first disciple!"
Hands folded, Anand spoke again
"O Tathagata, I also want what you want.
Getting rid of this tattered body is my goal too.
I also want to get my soul released from this coffin."
Buddha said, "I know how you feel, Anand.
You feel that if I am going to change my apparel
why can't you do it? Is that so, my man?"
"Yes, Master," Anand said.
"Mistaken you are, O' my chosen disciple
you are but sadly mistaken.
No, right now I am not getting my release from the birth cycle.
I have yet to have one more birth."
"What kind of birth, O my revered Master?" Afraid that Buddha
would just sink back into his *samadhi*,
Anand asked this question in a hurry.
But Buddha spoke, clearly and meaningfully.
"It would be a life span in which all of you
who are my disciples now
would be my disciples once again.
All of you would forsake me.
You would deny my faith and call me an imposter.
You would let me be put on the cross and be crucified.
And then . . . ." Buddha's voice sank but momentarily.
"My disciples, all of you, would agree
not with me, but with my crucifiers.
You would leave me upon others' mercy to be jilted .

. . . but as I said, that span would be my last life.
The crucifixion that I couldn't get in this life
I will get in the next life."
"What would be your next birth, Master?"
Buddha hesitated, but just for a moment.
"I would be known as Jesus!" he said,
"But he's to be
five centuries hence from now. You' can't hear of him now."
Was there really a smile on Buddha's lips or Anand just guessed?

*   *   *

Reflections and Reminiscences

SOUL OR A NOISELESS PATIENT SPIDER

I read Walt Whitman's poem A *Noiseless Patient Spider*when I was just thirteen. I memorized it and let it evolve and revolve in my mind. The question I asked myself was, if the world 'soul' in it is replaced by 'poem', will it not be more appropriate? Let's now read the poem.

A noiseless patient spider,
I mark'd where on a little promontory it stood isolated,
Mark'd how to explore the vacant cast surrounding,
It launch'd forth filament, filament, filament, out of itself,
Ever unreeling them, every tirelessly speeding them.
And you O my soul where you stand,
Surrounded, detached, in measureless oceans of space,
Ceaselessly musing, venturing, throwing, seeking the spheres to connect them
Till the bridge you will need be form'd, till the ductile anchor hold,
Till the gossamer thread you fling catch, somewhere, O my soul.
Today, 67 years later, I feel that I wasn't wrong. If Walt Whitman had been born in this century, he would certainly have used the metaphor of the spider's web for his creative urge to write a poem rather than the amorphous nomenclature 'soul'.

Satyapal Anand

Comparisons, they say (and rightly!) are odious. Occasionally I feel like smelling this odious aroma. One way to do it is to compare and contrast, not two persons, but two categories, *viz.*

63

Soul -mongering poets and soul-killing scientists and philosophers. As one of the first category I wrote umpteen poems in Urdu. In search of a soul (that I perforce already had somewhere in the labyrinths of my corporeal body) I wrote lines that bordered on an amalgam of sense and nonsense.

"Teach me to drink creation whole …. And casting out, myself, become a soul," was one such line. "There is one spectacle grander than the sea that is the sky; there is one spectacle grander than the sky that is the interior of the soul." Yet philosophers like Santayana would opine: "All spiritual interests are supported by animal life."

Of late (yet not very late either) Buddhist influence is now becoming increasingly evident virtually everywhere on the contemporary religious-cultural scene. I am afraid of touching Islamic neo-thought that borders on a retreat to the early centuries of "all that ensues forth from the holy book". However, even Judaism has somehow found kinship with Buddhism – in a way one would not have thought it was possible. Rodger Kamenerz's book *The Jew in the Lotus* affirms the relevance of Buddhist thought and practice for modern Jews. Motivational seminars emphasizing elements of Buddhist thought attract *mystical experience* and *business success.* (What a combination, indeed!) Already, as early as 1985, John Heider's *The Tao of Leadership* popularized for the business community the thoughts of the 5th century Chinese sage Lao-Tzu.

In 2001, I came across the August edition of *O: The Oprah Magazine.* It featured an upbeat interview with the Dalai Lama. Oprah asks if "there wasn't part of you that had always known you were different?" The Dalai Lama replies, "Sometimes I do feel that, yes, I may feel some effect of previous lives…..I have had glimpses of memory from past lives in which I identify with those from, in some cases, one or two centuries ago, I once had the feeling that may have been in Egypt 600 years so.

In 1999 when the Dalai Lama's book *Ethics for the New Millennium* was published I was down with a fell disease and had temporarily migrated to Canada for rest and restoration of my bruised body. I bought a copy by mail. I learnt that it had sold, for continuous eight weeks, more than any other book in recent years. (In fact the Dalai Lama has produced a steady stream of popular books for Western readers over the past many years). His recent titles include "*Transforming the Mind*", "*The Art of Happiness*" and "*The Path to Tranquility*". Even the Dalai Lama's mother (now 95 years old) has become an author of note with her recent release of "*My Son: A Mother's Story*", which is co-edited by her grandson, Khedroob Thondup.

Going back to Walt Whitman's verse ….

And you O my soul where you stand,
Surrounded, detached, in measureless oceans of space,
Ceaselessly musing, venturing, throwing, seeking the spheres to connect them
Till the bridge you will need be form'd, till the ductile anchor hold,
Till the gossamer thread you fling catch, somewhere, O my soul.
Soul is, thus, the new frontier for the seeker in America as is the ultimate reaches of universe for the space program…

*   *   *

IS LIFE FAIR?

Pramod, elder of my two sons, saddled with a multiplicity of problems, was rather in a pensive mood that day. A couple of years back, when I was staying with Pramod and his family in Canada, we were sitting in the living room of Manoj Sachdeva's house with a couple of other guests and having an after-dinner chat. Talking about what Pramod called the bad cards fate deals to some people, he had said – "Life isn't fair; it is just bumbling along dealing a good or a bad hand without knowing who deserves what."

I had earlier quoted from Guru Nanak's verse in *Japuji Saheb*....
Sochian soch na hoviei, je sochey lukh war...
and ended the shlokawith
"Sehs sianpan lukh hoven, tan ik na challey naal",
(One cannot think of the ultimate even if one were to try a million times: Even if one traverse a hundred ways of wisdom not even one may be the true one.).

To this comment of mine, another guest at this gathering, a Sikh Doctor or a Sikh Lady Doctor's husband (I don't know who!) had talked about good *karma* always getting good results and bad *karma* invariably getting bad results. Pramod's comments, pensive as these were, had come from him with a deep sigh that tore my heart asunder.

I suddenly heard myself saying, "Who said life was going to be fair, or that it was even meant to be fair? Guru Nanak didn't mean that. Let's begin with this supposition that life isn't fair. .. And the sooner we come to terms with this unpalatable truth, better it would be for us."

Having said that I suddenly realized that this was not a dictum that I had always held dear to my heart; it was something that I thought of there and then. Indeed, it went against the very grain of my approach to life. Nodding my head remorsefully I thought that I had changed, for better or for worse, I didn't know, but I may have to revise it later.

I am today rethinking of what I had said then – and how much of it I nourish as an unpleasant truth even today when life has dealt me one bad card after another – so much so, that the pack now doesn't have a single card left – good or bad. One of the mistakes many of us make is that we feel sorry for ourselves, or for others, thinking that life should be fair, or that some day it will be.

Well, my precious readers, it's **not** and it **won't.**

When we make this mistake we tend to spend a lot of time wallowing in grief and complaining about what's wrong with life. "It's not fair," we complain, not realizing that, perhaps, it was never intended to be. One of the nice things about surrendering to the fact that life isn't fair is that it keeps us from feeling sorry for ourselves by encouraging us to do the very best we can with what we have.

The fact that life isn't fair doesn't mean we shouldn't do everything in our power to improve our own lives or the world around us. To the contrary, it suggests that we should. Self pity, indeed, is a defeating emotion that does nothing for anyone, except to make us more miserable than we actually are.

If you are an avid reader of Urdu *ghazal* poetry, you would know that the large corpus of literature is just one big bundle of the luxury of grief in which the poet, his readers, his listeners in the *mushairas,* and their coming generations wallow. It is like taking a bath in a medicinal mud, coming out soiled in body but clean in spirit.

The Urdu poet, of course, weeps for himself, either bound by tradition or bound by his own condition, but always with crocodile tears. Of course, one cannot weep for the entire world. It is beyond human strength so the Urdu poets choose to weep for themselves.

In Talmud, a holy verse says: "The deeper the sorrow, the less tongue it hath." That is silent weeping, my friends, for as William Blake says, "Excessive sorrow laughs: excessive joy weeps."

The next time, my dear readers, you find yourself thinking about the injustices of the world or fate or both, try reminding yourself of this very basic fact. You may be surprised that it can nudge you out of self-pity and into helpful action....So here is the key word...action, i.e. *karma*, and remember what Lord Krishna says in Geeta, *tu karm kar, aur phal ki aasha na rakh. Phal mujh par chhor dey.* (Do your *karma* and don't hope for its reward. Let the reward-giving be my prerogative).

Hazrat Ali also says in one of his rarest gems of wisdom: "Blessed is the one who never expects any reward for doing his duty, for he shall never be disappointed."

Leaving my readers with this quip-like quote from Hazrat Ali, let me confide in them, that these days I am engrossed in reading Hazrat Ali's sayings, and let me say with hindsight that he is one of the best practical philosophers the world has produced.

*   *   *

AM I SUICIDAL?

Alternating between bouts of depression and high spirits, both bad for my mental health, I have often thought that if my depression gets worse, I might commit suicide or if the anti-depression medicines get hold of me, I might murder someone. Let me see what choices I have. I vacillate between depression and (to coin a term) *hipression* (*hi* is Greek for 'high'). I might commit suicide if *de* is not controlled; in case of *hi*, I might commit a murder.

Let us see if any of my tribe of scribes has done either of these acts. Novelist Virginia Woolf, who wrote *"A Room of One's Own"* and *"To the Lighthouse"*, had depression and she drowned herself as a cruelly symbolic measure of judging watery stream of consciousness. Fairytale author Hans Christian Andersen, who wrote *"The Ugly Duckling"* and *"The Little Mermaid"*, had depression and thrice tried to end his life. Russian author Gogol shut himself in a room and starved himself to death. Count Leo Tolstoy died of hyperthermia by sitting through a snow storm for the whole night on a railway station bench. (I wrote a poem about it and wished to die likewise.)USA author and journalist Ernest Hemingway, who wrote *"For Whom the Bell Tolls"*, in a fit of depression, shot himself. Urdu poets, egged on by a desire of self-annihilation, who chose to drink themselves to death are no fewer than fifty even in modern times.

My latest couplet in Urdu shows this desire with a stark black-and-white background. Here it is: *MaiN dekh sakuN apney na honey ka tamaasha: A chara-gar tabeeb, mujhey la-ilaaj kar: (tr. O my helpful physician, make my ailment irremediable: For I want to see the state of my non-being.*

What is so enjoyable in the moment of death that one wants to savor its taste with relish? They say that there is a delight in fancy, but imagine the actual *moment of death,* how does one 'taste' it with all the five senses dying one by one? No one has come back to life to tell us about it. I have a feeling that if there are poets in heaven or hell, they would be writing about the exact moment when they departed this world of misery.

We both suffer from the same alternating bouts of depression and *'hipression'* – yes, both - Saqi Farooqi and I. We compare our notes often. He phones me from London and I tell him how near or far I am from suicidal longings. I phone him and tell him that it is a long, dark, winding tunnel from which one has to escape, come what may or one will be buried under. I tell him the medicine I have been prescribed. He tells me of his own poison (Drinking is now an anathema for him.) One stark difference between us is that there is Gundi, his wife, to mourn him – (what a feeling of satisfaction, after one dies!) but there is no one in my case – (what a feeling of dismay, after one is dead! Sheila, the German born wife of Noon Meem Rashid, the celebrated Urdu poet, is reported to have told our common friends in London, that on innumerable occasions, Rashid would indulge in the luxury of grief by thinking of committing suicide. (He always wished to die in the arms of a woman!) So would Saqi and I both if we had the boon of a pair of loving arms to hold us tight when we cease breathing.

Recently BBC came up with a story about creative people more prone to insanity, bi-polar disorders and suicidal tendencies. Please see this excerpt.

Byron was "mad, bad and dangerous to know", according to one of his lady loves, Keats was driven to distraction by obsessive love and Sylvia Plath ended her own life. Depression, madness and insanity are themes which have run throughout the history of poetry. The incidence of mood disorders, suicide and mental asylum stay was 20 times higher among major British and Irish poets between 1600 and 1800 according to a study by psychologist

Kay Redfield Jamison. In other words, poets are 20 times more likely to end up in an asylum than the general population.

As far back as the mid 1800s, Emily Dickinson stated that "much madness is the divines' sense" and Edgar Allan Poe questioned "whether madness is or is not the loftiest intelligence".

"Part of poetry is making words do more work that they usually should do and so you're looking for every angle of what a word might mean and so your brain starts working like as well - over-analyzing everything and zooming in to minute detail."

So, friends, if tomorrow you get the news that Satyapal Anand has risen to constellation of suicide prone poets, don't be surprised!

*　　*　　*

THE HEN OR THE EGG? SCIENCE – A REASONABLE ABSURDITY

When I was a school student at the 5th grade level, History and Geography were bundled up as one subject called "General Knowledge". It had some elements of rudimentary science as well. The medium of teaching was Urdu. In the next grade 'Science' was a compulsory subject. Our teacher was an old man with a funny name, Jhanda Singh. We called him *Jhanda Danda* in his absence as he was a very strict teacher. Scientific laws, he told us in his Urdu mixed with Punjabi and English, were infallible. "The laws, {to translate his Peshawari idiom into today's English), were infallible. They were fixed from the moment of cosmic birth, imprinted on the universe like a maker's signature…and the universe was governed by universal, mathematically precise laws which were immutable, absolute and dependable."

The theory of 'big bang' he knew something about. He told us, gesticulating wildly with his hands, a flowing beard and a loosely tied turban, that there was an explosion of cosmic dimensions, and lo and behold, stars and planets were thrown off into the limitless ether like burning whirlwinds. Solidified over eons, they became today's suns and earths. It was indeed an awe-inspiring visual scene that we, the 11 and 12 year old boys, conjured up in our minds.

At home, we the Muslim or Hindu or Sikh boys had learnt something different about the birth of the cosmos. To me, a Hindu, it was Brahma who brought about the birth (*utpati*). It was Vishnu who sustains and nurtures it, and Shiva who brings about destruction. To the Muslims as also to the Christians, it was a different story. Adam and Eve were created and then transported to the Garden of Eden. The story of Eve's fall at the behest of Satan and then Adam's act of disobedience, and the beginning of a family was almost the same, with a little difference here and there for Christian and Muslim boys. So there was a diametrically opposed view point between faith and science.

Today I know much more about the laws of electromagnetism, the laws that regulate the world within the atom, the laws of motion – expressed as tidy mathematical relationship. But where do these laws come from? Did someone formulate these for us? If so, who? And for what purpose did he do it? I have personally known some brilliant scientists who go through their daily *Puja* at home or as Muslims observe the *Muharram* fasting, and yet in their labs and classrooms they teach the infallible laws (or suppositions?) of science.

Ask me why the laws of physics are what they are - and I have no answer except that there is no reason; they are what they are, and have always been there. In USA, where I teach now, some Catholic majority states have brought about – what they call – *The Intelligent Design.* To them, the cause or a reason why is there. There has to be a beginning point. Nothing is made without a maker. *The Intelligent Design,* to them is the bedrock foundation on which the superstructure of science is built.

It is in this context that I must talk a little about my grandson Asher. He's eleven years old and till he was eight or nine, always began his conversation "You don't know anything Dada ji," Even now while he doesn't say it, he means something like that by his demeanor and then launches into a lengthy discussion of why Pluto has been taken out of the fraternity of planets, or how do the fish breathe under water or why do earthquakes come under water. An ignoramus and fussy old man that I presume I am, this eleven years old prodigy knows much more than I knew even at the age of fifteen. So, let's presume that our schools, TV channels like Animal Planet, Discovery or educational comics teach much more of Science than the religions would ever do of the Intelligent Design.

Intelligent Design or no Intelligent Design, if I say that science is rooted in reasonable absurdity, wouldn't it be right? I can go a step further and say that it is a bit of clever, if not cruel, joke that someone has played on us. Let me now close this short piece with a couplet or Urdu. *Takhleeq-kayanat ke dilchasp jurm par / Hansta to ho ga aap bhi yazdan kabhi kabhi!* (The creator would indeed be laughing sometimes in His sleeves at his own bewitching crime of having created the universe!)

*   *   *

MIDNIGHT – 23-24 APRIL 1564

Twirled around the neck of the baby
Was the maternal cord
As if the new-born had reached the end of his life
Even before he was born ...
But ...
The midwife was an expert
She got up
Looking for a pair of scissors
She went around the room
Couldn't find one
So she bent and reached down
The blood soaked cord she cut with
Her teeth
Removed the entanglement
Freed the tiny neck from the noose
The baby shuddered a little
Whimpered as if he was complaining
...
"What does the world need me for?
How would it gain if I live?
I'm but an ordinary human baby
That's what I am!
The baby said to himself."
The midwife said to the mother
"Here hold your William, young mom
The baby's clean now
Doesn't he look cute?"

$*$ $*$ $*$

That was a poem I wrote first in Urdu and then translated it into English for inclusion in one of my five books of English poems published recently. The Notes I appended with the poem were:

Shakespeare was born, midnight 23-24 April, 1564.
Satyapal Anand was born the same night 367 years later.
Both had to undergo the same cord-cutting rigmarole.

I had no idea that with its publication not in a literary journal but in a book would attract so much healthy and 'unhealthy' criticism by readers and reviewers. I got a plethora of emails forwarded to me by my agent as also comments on Face book.

Some of these are very interesting. Since there is no legal bar in reproducing them here, I venture forth and do it with impunity that, some say, is the hallmark of my writing.

John Hollinger from London wrote, "Hindus are always keen to know about their previous birth cycles. When I was in India, I was taken by a Hindu friend of mine to an astrologer who told me that I was born a *Yahoodi* (Jew) in *Roos* (Russia) and that I was put in a gas chamber and killed. When? I asked him. He said after some calculation, "About seventy years ago, sir. May be, I don't know. The period your 'atman' was in a void before your present birth, I cannot calculate," Later, my friend told me that the astrologer was an illiterate man, and when it came to European history or the holocaust, he would know next to nothing." How did he divine the fact of German gassing of Jews, he didn't know.... So, does Mr. Anand think..." John Hollinger asked in his email, "...that he is Shakespeare reborn, and that for four centuries Shakespeare's soul has been wandering in the void?"

Kamala Kapadia wrote from Jaipur, India. "Hilarious it is, indeed, Mr. Anand! I have no exact statistics but I can assure that all over the world thousands of babies are born each year on 23rd April midnight. All these babies ..... Are they reincarnations of Shakespeare? Be reasonable, Mr. Anand; don't be a poetic buffoon to claim that status.....The historical fact of the maternal cord being would around the neck is, however, something novel for I never read that about Shakespeare."

Matthew Shanks wrote from Chicago. "Good! I know poets have always something in common. Shakespeare reincarnated– and you? A python and a worm, what a comparison! Why don't you write plays like Shakespeare, man?"

My friend Dr. Sadiq Husain wrote from Pakistan, "The more I read your book *One Hundred Buddhas,* the more I tend to believe in the phenomenon of transmigration of souls. Being a Muslim my belief and my logic seem to be in conflict here. Could it be that Shakespeare's soul went through a long cycle of births and rebirths in the 367 years, you say, elapsed between his birth and yours? What an idea!"

The best (or the worst) comment came from a man (Joshua Young), once again from London. "You are, Sir, a Falstaff as also all Shakespearean clowns rolled into one, because you have their bluff, their wisdom wrapped up in tomfoolery and their sharp tongue. I wish I could see you in person to know if you dress up also like a Shakespearean fool."

Well, it seems that the more reviews of my book are published (almost every week there is a new one while old ones include one even in *The Guardian,* London), more fan mail or hate mail is likely to follow. Interesting? Isn't it?

*   *   *

A 'DESI' IN A THREE-PIECE SUIT

'Desi' (indigenous) – indeed, I am, in all aspects of my being. A strong Punjabi build, complexion, look, temper and food habits notwithstanding, in my speech I revert to chaste Urdu or equally chase Hindi or rustic Punjabi once I am back in my own flock. It is always a story from *to-to- fro*, and not *to* and *fro*. So when I got a call from a publisher who wanted me to get as many books of poetry in English as I liked (but all before the bell tolled on the close of 2011), I dug up all my old and new poems originally written in English or Urdu that I thought would go well in English garb for the Yankees here in America. I took fewer than 150 days that is five months, to cull them up, put all of them in a three-piece suit – complete with bow and tie, and presented them in five volumes of English poetry. Some of them were not worthy of the three-piece-suit for they were of the inner city tribe. So I put them in a pair of loose, torn jeans and faded shirt and gave them the *albino* brand of American English to speak their innards out.

Miracle it was, wasn't it?

Yes, but a miracle wrought with 'hard labour' inside my study room – 10 to 14 hours of work every day, shaking, whisking, beating, churning up word and phrase, verse and rhyme, alliterative concoctions, sometimes massacring grammar in a cruel mood, piecing prose to draw out the essential pathetic and poignant poetic element in its true heart – and then writing my poems in English.

Believe my sworn statement, my friends and readers! I wrote as many as 320 poems in English, typed them out with ten arthritis-effected fingers and my publishers were always one step ahead of me, culling up my typed work straight from my computer to their editors, being in telephonic contact with me ten times (or more) a day. Five books of poetry were published in fewer than as many months. And what kind of books! Beautiful to look at and hold them in your hand, a *desideratum,* an asset to put them in front of you on the bookshelf, look at them and be happy that **you** had written them.

So, it wasn't a miracle. It was neither Sisyphus's meaningless labour nor a Samson-sans-hair bringing down the portals of the city. There was no Delilah in the background except for an ardent wish of mine to see *Urdu as a world language tall enough to be seen as a junior partner in the world assembly of languages.*

Disappointed occasionally I was when even well-read poets in an organization of poets in Washington D.C., I was asked, point-blank, such a bland question, as "What is Urdu, Dr. Anand?" I felt like a homeless man. I did my best to tell them that Urdu was a language. Where was it spoken – like Spanish in Spain, French in France, German in Germany, Danish in Denmark? That was the moot point – no, less than a moot point, because Urdu doesn't have a country to tag itself to – at least with its name and nomenclature. Explain you may, as much as you can, but statistics say that not more than five to ten per cent people speak Urdu in Pakistan, a country that is supposed to enshrine it as its official language. About India, less said is always better. Because the language is, more often than not, Urdu, but the tag is Hindi.

I was, however, more than happy about the response. It was the "book season" – yes, that is what it was. In USA, Christmas is the time when people give gifts to their loved ones, and books are on top of the list– dresses and cosmetics come next. In our homeland, books are not even a commodity; if a book is given as a present, the recipient feels let down rather than elated. And thereby hangs a tale.

So, as I was saying, it was the book season, and quite a few bundles were sold. Not to my countrymen, only a few (count them in a single digit) bought my books, but there were the common American folk who did and did it in triple figure.

I am rather late in giving the titles of the five books in this write-up. These are *(1) The Dream Weaver, (2) A Vagrant Mirror, (3) One-Hundred Buddhas, (4) Sunset Strands, and (5) If Winter comes.*

Except for *One-Hundred Buddhas* which has forty poems and as many full-page icon-images of Buddha, all others have about 70 poems each, taking the total to plus-three hundred.

*   *   *

A FUNNY QUID-PRO-QUO

It is indeed inappropriate to say that old photographs smell musty, stale, fetid and sour. To me, they bring the sweet-sour memories of the day when these were taken. I hardly ever open old albums but when I do, I spend hours re-living the moments with dear and near ones who people the photographs in these albums. Someone said that photography records the gamut of feelings written

I still have my father's daily diary in Urdu in which he wrote about important events as reported in *The Tribune*, Lahore. An entry in 1932 refers to Lala Diblagh Rai, a professor of history in D.A.V.College, Lahore. He presented a research paper in a meeting of Hindu elders held in the Lakshmi Insurance Building. This 'research paper' was later published in *The Tribune*. Lala Dilbagh Rai wrote that the credit of the discovery of South American continent must go to a Hindu sea voyager and religious missionary named Arjun Das. He claimed that Argentina had been named after Arjun Das.

My father's diary also notes the reaction in the Muslim academicians and journalists of Lahore at the time. It has this noteworthy comment, *"Maulana Zafar Ali Khan Ne akhbar Rozana "Zamindar" mein Lala Ji ke mazmoon ka mazaq udaya aur likha ki yeh aysey hi hai ki jaisey hum likhen ki Janoobi America aik Muslim jahazran, Sheikh Chilly ne daryaft kia tha, kionke whan Chile nam ka ek mulk hai."* (Maulana Zafar Ali Khan wrote a satirical article in the daily *Zamindar* saying that this claim was like Muslims saying that South America was discovered by a Muslim Voyager named Sheikh Chilli because there's a country by that name there).

A few pages later, my father notes down various letters to the editor of both *The Tribune* and the daily *Zamindar (Urdu)*

that support or counteract this claim. One detailed letter is from a Christian scholar Joshua Fazal Din of Lahore published in Urdu daily *Zamindar*. His approach is candid and impartial. He debunks such silly theories as Germany having taken the secrets of scientific inventions from the holy books of the Hindus or about the origin of the name of Argentina. Nonetheless, he talks about the all-enveloping, corrupting influence of Hindu customs on sister religions in India in terms of what he calls *chote-par-chote muqabila* i.e. blow-by-blow competition.

I now translate this Urdu letter as quoted in my father's diary.

"My whole family was adherent to Islam. We got converted to Christianity. Now, as a Christian, when I cast an impartial look at both Hindus and Muslims, I find that there is a competition in claims of equality or superiority in many fields. There are some fairs, festivals and holy days in the Muslim Calendar which are privy only to India and or nothing but carbon copies of Hindu festivals. To offset *Janam Ashtami,* Muslims started celebrating the birthday of the Prophet, known as *Jashn-i-Meelad-i-Nabi* with fanfare. This festival is celebrated in no other country except India. For *Diwali*, Muslims now have 'shab-i-baraat', a festival about which there is no record of fanfare and celebration before the 20th century. Such customs as *daaj* (dowry) are now a part and parcel of Muslim marriages. They call it *jahez*. For Nikah, (marriage) they now have countless intricate customs and practices borrowed from the Hindus, such as *sehra, ghorey par sawar nosha, dulhan-dikhaii* (sehra, the groom riding a horse, bride showing ceremony) that are the same as practiced by the Hindus."

It is a long letter and Joshua Fazal Din is not partial to either of the two religions, their customs and the prevalent habit of 'holier than thou' approach. Which of the two is higher on the totem pole of customs is the order of the day? He seems to be asking.

Well, I wonder if today's Pakistan and India are not following the same pattern and pace of a blow-for-blow in national and international politics.

*   *   *

ALL ABOUT MY CHILDREN

"We find delight in the beauty and
happiness in children that makes the
heart too big for the body."

Chats with my children

Letters to Pramod, Daisy & Sachin

EYE OF THE STORM

We all know what the eye of a storm is. It is the peaceful area around which a whirlwind is blowing in full swing. It is a safe rounded pocket around which the storm is howling with full force. The tornado is sweeping around in full force but the 'eye' is quiet and peaceful.

How nice it would be if we too could be calm and serene in the midst of chaos – in the eye of the storm!

Surprisingly enough, it's much easier than you might imagine it to be in the eye of a "human storm". I learnt the trick after experimenting with it a number of times. All my life, I had the habit of jumping into the very center of the storm of a discussion, debate, heated argument. I would become a 'party', a 'partisan', a committed person to one side and thus open to onslaughts by the other side. Now, pretty late in life, I have learnt the 'trick' of remaining in the eye of the human storm till I find the most appropriate moment to step calmly into the debate.

Suppose you are going to a family gathering that is likely to be chaotic. You can tell yourself that you are going to use the experience as an opportunity to remain calm. You can commit to being the one person in the room who will be an example of peace to others. You can practice breathing while others are shouting. You can practice listening. You can let others be right and enjoy their glory of that moment. You can do it if you set your mind to it.

In the house of your Mom's eldest sister in Jabalpur (10 members of the family when I visited it in 1975), every one spoke loudly, nay, almost at the top of their voices. I asked the husband of my wife's elder sister, the head of the family, how one could make others hear him in that din. He smiled and said, "I use a trick. When everybody is shouting, I keep quiet. Then choosing a moment I say something in undertones, almost a whisper. My whisper is out of tune in the top range of their mutual bickering, and, therefore, they all hear it. Then they become relatively quiet, and it is then and then only that I give my opinion."

By starting out with harmless scenarios like family gathering, cocktail parties, and birthday parties for children, you can build a track record and enjoy some success. You'll notice that by being in the eye of the storm, you will be more present-moment oriented. Once you have practiced (and mastered it) in the microcosm of your own family, you can practice on more difficult areas of life – dealing with conflict, hardship, or grief. If you start slowly, have some success, and keep practicing, pretty soon you'll know how to live in the eye of the storm.

My precious children! Please do not think, even for a moment, that I am preaching what I don't practice myself. I have been wrong all of my life in shouting, letting others know and acknowledge my presence, and it was only in the last two years that I have learnt this technique. I am writing these missives to you only because I want you not to learn these hard truths of life the hard way I have.

*   *   *

NEVER INSIST ON PROVING YOUR POINT

I used to brag about myself a lot. Whenever, in a meeting or a social gathering, some people gathered around me and I was expected to give my opinion about a matter, I would always begin with my 'shining' autobiographical details. Gradually (and painfully) I learnt that this was the surest way of alienating people. *Jo zarra jis jagah hai, wahin aaftab hai,* جو ذرّہ جس جگہ ہے، وہیں آفتاب ہے۔ says the Urdu proverb. A dust particle, wherever it is, is in itself a sun.

So I reached the conclusion that humility and inner peace go hand in hand. The less compelled one is to try to prove one to others, the easier it is to feel peaceful inside. It is a dangerous trap to prove your point. It takes an enormous amount of energy to be continually pointing out your accomplishments, bragging, or trying to convince others of your worth. Bragging actually dilutes the positive feelings you receive from an accomplishment or something you are proud of. To make matters worse, the more you try to prove your point, the more others will avoid you, talk behind your back about your insecure need to brag, and perhaps even resent you.

I gradually discovered that people are drawn to those with a quiet, inner confidence, people who don't need to make themselves look good, be "right" all the time, or steal the glory. Most people love a person who doesn't need to brag, a person who shares from his or her heart not from his or her ego.

Years ago, while flying from London to Delhi I had a seat to share with an elderly couple who were conversing in chaste Urdu.

Since they were busy in themselves, I sat quietly and then took out an Urdu magazine from my handbook and started reading it. After some time, I felt their inquisitive eyes focused on me. Then the husband politely asked me, "Do you know Urdu, sir?" I smiled and said, "Well, I do....I love Urdu." The conversation rested at that point and I kept on reading the journal till I came to a page where one of my poems was published with my photograph and my name. I was about to turn the page when I found the man's hand on my hand. "Don't turn the page, Doctor Anand; Let me read your poem."

I gave the magazine to him. He said almost reverently, "I knew all the time that I had seen you somewhere....and then when I saw your picture I discovered that I had never seen you in person, but only in pictures...I mean your pictures in Urdu magazines."

Slow learner that I am let me confess that all my life I have been a bragger, and it was only a few years back that I learnt the art of good judgment and humility. So, my children take a cue from my mistakes and never insist on proving a point in a social group. Try humility.

*   *   *

ANGST ABOUT SMALL MATTERS

A stranger today cut in front of my friend when he was driving with me in the back seat. Rather than let it go, and go on with his day, he seemed convinced that he was justified in his anger. He shouted "Asshole!" within hearing not only of his wife and me, but also his son just six years old. I thought about it later. He seemed to have, in a split second, played out an imaginary confrontation in his mind with the other driver and finding him at fault, hurled the profanity at him. Did it satisfy my son? No, he kept on boiling, of course, in undertones, for another minute or two.

Why not instead simply allow the driver to have his accident somewhere else? Try to have compassion for the person and remember how painful it is to be in such an enormous hurry. Maybe, his wife was in the hospital or his child was unwell and he had to reach him.

There are many similar, unimportant irritants, which hold us for a while from our straight course. Whether we had to wait in line, listen to unfair criticism, or do the lion's share of the work, it pays enormous dividends if we learn not to worry about little things. So many people spend so much of their life energy "sweating the small stuff" that they completely lose touch with the magic and beauty of life. When you commit to working toward this goal, you will find that you will have far more energy to be kinder and gentler.

(For Sachin, in particular)

*   *   *

PPP - Patience, Practice, Period

I have been one of the tribe of go-getters all my life. Starting from rags after coming from Pakistan, it is not a story of sudden rise to riches. If I could educate myself and sustain a family, this probably was due to my tireless labor and zeal to reach the top in every conceivable way. Work, work, work, zeal, zeal, zeal, ardor and eagerness, eagerness, eagerness, enthusiasm, enthusiasm, enthusiasm – these have been my watch words all my life. Now, however, when I look back, I find that this act of undue hurry, this urge to forge forward, this attitude of not to run along, but run ahead, has been my doing and undoing both. I lost a number of friends who were left behind. I lost a number of prospective friends who were ahead of me and perforce lagged behind me thereby losing love for me. On the other hand, I could rise to the top in my chosen profession, i.e. teaching, and in my chosen field of action, i.e. Urdu literature.

Now, when I am retired I feel that I couldn't keep balance between the two – the ardor and enthusiasm on the one hand and patience, endurance and calm on the other. So, what I am practicing now is the triple "Ps", Patience through Practice /Period.

What I now do every day is easy. You also can start doing it with as little as five minutes and build up your capacity for patience, over time. Start by saying to yourself, "Okay, for the next five minutes I won't allow myself to be bothered by anything. I will b e patient." This, as you already know, is Maun (silence absolute) as they call it in *Yog Sadhna*. (The Yoga Practice). What you'll discover is truly amazing. Your intention to be patient, especially if you know it's only for a short while, immediately strengthens your capacity for patience. Hurry and impatience, as you know, feed on themselves. Once you reach little milestones – five minutes of successful patience – you'll begin to see that you do, indeed, have the capacity to be patient, even for longer periods of time. Over time, you'll become a patient person.

You see, now from an angry person, always in a hurry to set the next person right and thus eventually set the whole world right, I have become a patient person almost in one year that I started practicing this branch of yoga. Being patient allows me to keep my perspective. I can remember, even in the midst of a difficult situation, that what's before me, my present challenge, isn't "life or death" but simply a minor obstacle that must be dealt with, not there and then, but later in a patient way, at a patient moment.

Will it make you sad if I tell you that I was once turned out of the house, by a very dear grown up young lady, one of my own kith and kin. With her hand raised, her eyes flashing – these were her words, "Get out of my house, now, at this very moment!"

For long periods of time after that event, I have re-lived this hellish moment in my mind till I met a saint at Rishikesh and told him my dilemma. He said, "Sit quietly for five minutes now, and keep on saying loudly for me to hear, "I have forgiven the person for all times to come." I obeyed his order. He told me that whenever the bitter memory of that moment comes to me, I should sit quietly and repeats this sentence as many times as I can. He also told me to cultivate that person with more kindness, affection, love, and selflessness than I do other friends and family members. I have been doing that, and I believe I have succeeded.

So, my very precious children, can you begin this practical yoga today by giving yourself five minutes of silence absolute i.e. "*Maun*" (Sanskrit) and tell yourselves I will be patient throughout today.

*   *   *

Groovy Growing

Do parents also grow alongside their children? I think they do. They're not aware of their own growth in terms of how they change from a childless marriage unit to a multiple family unit, but they do indeed change. They have to cut, alter, and re-stitch the apparel of their personal, familial, social and financial life to suit the begetting of one or two or three more mouths, mouths that cry to be fed. This change borders almost on mutation, on metamorphosis, even on a re-birth for parents themselves.

We both went through this change. I can't divine anything about your mom for she started remaining unwell soon after Sharpy's birth, but I found (nay, at that moment in time I didn't find – but now I do!) myself changing. I was indeed under a lot of stress, working no fewer than 12 hours a day, managing to run errands for the household, doing everything reasonably well within my means – and sometimes unreasonably outside my means. This told upon my nature. When winter comes in US or Canada, we all weatherproof our houses, fixing cracks and holes and making our homes safe. Well, it was a kind of winter but without knowing I failed to winter proof the home that was my own self, my nature, my disposition.

I knew much depended on me for mom was but a stay-at-home mom. For as long as two years that we were in the D-type house, the only escape for me became a trip with Mr. Bedi to Sector 22, almost every working day. It took as much as two hours for me to return home. I knew it was rather a stress pattern that I was weaving both for myself and for mom because what I could do for the kids for the school assignments, she couldn't, but I kept it up,

I don't know why. I gave up writing in Urdu and Hindi altogether, gave up going to *Mushairas* and *Mehfils*, for I had to earn the extra rupee for a hundred different needs. However, on Sundays I made good the shortfall in devotion of my time to the family, by taking all of them to Sector 17 for window shopping and coffee house jaunt.

After a two years' stay in D/4, when we moved to E-1/92, my routine changed. My friendship with Bedi got less warm and I stopped going to Sector 22 with him. So, each evening, all of us went to Sector 15 *rehri* (shopping cart) market for vegetables and sundry groceries. We walked a distance of a little more than a mile each way. On our way back, burdened with bags and baskets, we chose to walk through the grounds but once Daisy had a foot sprain and then we chose never to take a short cut. Bubby sometimes went with his friends and missed this jaunt, but Daisy and Sharpy were our constant companions. When Sharpy got tired of walking, he would look up at me and impeach me to pick him up and let him ride on my shoulders. He would just say *"chucho!"* which meant, "Lift me up in your arms, please." I often did it, but I found a way to avoid it. So I would pose a challenge to the two of them to run fast and reach the next electric pole – and mutual competition kept them on their feet longer than I could hope for. Finally, I would carry him in my arms and he snuggled against me, tired and exhausted, indeed, a lovely bundle of love and warmth.

We both were changing alongside the growth of our children. Their growth and our decay went hand in hand as various ailments started afflicting us, more your mom than me, but I wasn't much of an exception, too.

*   *   *

NAMES, NICK-NAMES, PET-NAMES

I remember a quotation that I read somewhere, probably by Ambrose Bierce, or Oscar Wilde, that said: "For every man there is something in the vocabulary that would stick to him like a second skin. His enemies have only to find it. His friends know it like their own second skin." Well, I had no way to give myself a name. My father had given me a name soon after my birth. He told me that he had named me after Dr. Satya Pal, a Congress leader of Jalianwala Bagh Massacre fame in Amritsar. He was a co-patriot of Lala Lajpat Rai, I later learnt.

I was given another opportunity to re-name myself when I started writing poetry in Urdu. All Urdu poets had their pen-names. I chose "Shayiq", and then discarded it. Later my sister Shanta chose "Sham" for me. I discarded that also when I learnt that in Hindi it meant the black one. Damn it, I told myself, my own name is good enough for me. Satyapal Anand. There was a little oversight here. Satya + Chit + Anand, in Hinduism, are the *summum bonum* of all names of God. It can be abbreviated to Sachidananad also. In my case, however, "Pal" is an intruder. How do I get rid of it? I asked myself and then wrote a poem in Urdu titled مجھ کو اپنے نام سے چڑ ہے۔ *Mujh ko apney naam sey chir hai.* (I am irked by my name).

Yet another opportunity came my way when I took up US citizenship. I was asked point blank by the officer if I would like to change my name there and then and it would be accepted as my new name in all official records and I would be issued a certificate that Satyapal Anand and (the newly named person) are one and the same. I thought for a moment and then, lo and behold, I couldn't get rid of Pal. i.e. the one who keeps the Truth. It is a different story that I tell a lot of lies and my name is just the opposite of it. I hardly ever prove myself to be the "Keeper of Truth" as defined in the *Upanishads*.

Well, I look back to the day of my first acquaintance with your mom's name. I was told that her name was Parmila and that Bhaiya ji of Jabalpur had given her this name at her birth. Since your mom did not have any other official paper such as a school certificate or birth certificate, at the time of the submission of her Matriculation form (that I filled because it was in English), I asked her if she would prefer to be called "Promila" (it sounded rather 'fashionable' to me) and she said "yes". This was how her name came to be known.

Pramod was named by his mom. I wasn't consulted because the P sound was the first syllable of the word from Guru Granth Sahib and we had to find a word beginning with P. How did she hit upon the word "Pramod", I don't know, but we all called him Babbu, Bubby, Bob, and never much thought of his real name.

Who christened Daisy? Well, when she was born in Sector 21, my wife's nephew from Ghaziabad) was staying with us for his Matriculation examination. There was another young man named Diwedi who shared the accommodation in the extra room in this 10-marla house. Diwedi and I both taught Surinder his English. His poetry book had a poem in which there was a line "Daisies are scattered far and near..." Diwedi explained to Surinder that Daisy was a fresh flower and he also said that it was also a common name for girls in England. We started calling her Daisy – and when she was sent to Christ School, we filled her name as Daisy Anand for no one had ever thought of giving her another name.

Sharpy was born when we lived in Sector 15. My sister Krishna from Delhi and your Mom's sister Mohni had come down from Jabalpur for help. Mom gave the name "Sharpy" to the baby because she had seen another boy named "Sharpy" in Sector 22, a colleague's son. This colleague taught history in DAV College and we were on visiting terms. Since "S" was the sound from Guru

Granth Sahib's *shloke*, (verse). Mom and I both thought that my name Satya might have an echo in Sachin.

Well, my precious children, about the pet names that glorify various domestic animals, goat, pig and donkey, I need not write anything. You might get offended, if I do. I would rather reproduce here some quotable quotes from poets, philosophers, parodying penmen of sorts that might help you.

For every man there is some something in the vocabulary that would stick to him like a second skin. His enemies have only to find it. (Ambrose Bierce: "Oleaginous": *The Devil's Dictionary) 1881*-1911

Don't take action because of a name! A name is an uncertain thing. You can't count on it. (Bertolt Brecht, *A Man is a Man* (1927)

Names are but noise and smoke / Obscuring heavenly light. (Goethe. "Martha's Garden". *Faust. Part I.* (1808).tr. Philip Wayne.

Of all eloquence a nickname is the most concise; of all arguments the most unanswerable. (William Hazlitt. "On Nicknames". *Sketches and Essays* (1839).

The name of man is a numbing blow from which he never recovers. (Marshall MC Luhan *Understanding Media* (1964).

What is in name? That which we call a rose / By any other name would smell as sweet. (Shakespeare. *Romeo and Juliet* 1594-95. 2.2.43.)

*   *   *

FRAGRANCE OF OLD PHOTOGRAPHS

It is indeed inappropriate to say that old photographs smell musty, stale, fetid and sour. To me, they bring the sweet-sour memories of the day when these were taken. I hardly ever open old albums but when I do, I spend hours re-living the moments with dear and near ones who people the photographs in these albums. Someone said that photography records the gamut of feelings written on the human face and thus immortalizes a moment – indeed turning it into eternity.

I espy one such moment when I open an old family album. An array of black-and-white photographs stare me in the face. The first leaf has a picture of my marriage. Two strangers look at me with happy faces. Who are they? I ask myself. Well, myself and my consort of fifty years – who else could they be? Young, hopeful, unconcerned with what life has in store for them.....vexations, worries and what not, but there is another thing too that peeps from behind their eyes .....

Was it truthfulness, trust and honesty? I ask myself. Yes it was. Did they know, I ask myself again, what life had in store for them? No, I answer. They did not! I smile when I recall that this photograph was published in the prestigious daily The Tribune then published from Ambala with the caption, Renowned Urdu writer, Satyapal Anand and his bride Promila, who were married in Ludhiana.

I look at another picture. In the background is house # D/4 on the University campus. I am holding my son Bubby (quite tall for his fifth birthday) outside the gate. We are both broadly smiling.

I remember the photograph was taken by a young American lady who had come as a member of American Peace Corps and perchance had wished to attend the birthday party at my house. The photograph was taken by an instant camera, the first ever I had seen that ejected a black-and-white photograph in a jiffy after clicking it. How cute Bubby was! Well, he is very handsome now, but in a different way. God bless him.

Another set of pictures in the front lawn of house # E-1/92 on the campus brings to my mind my friend Krishan Adeeb who was a gifted photographer and had taken my children's photograph - Bubby and Daisy – and of course, the baby of the family, Sharpy.

What a set of pictures! What a treat it is to watch, in this picture, Sharpy's innocent, angelic face, still babyish at 6 years of age! I again remember his next door friend Sunil Mall. The two of them, eight and seven years old respectively, had driven away my friend Balwant Gargi's Impala Car parked outside our house and almost 'dumped' it into the garbage dump at the corner. Alas, Sunil is no more. The chain of memories brings back the face of his elder brother, a 6-years old kid, who liked Daisy very much. Sometimes he'd bring a flower for her and say: "I have plucked it for Daisy." The three brothers had no sister and naturally Daisy, the only girl next door, filled that gap.

Yet another picture! The lambretta scooter # RJK-56 has five riders. I am sitting on the driver's seat. Daisy is standing in the space between the handle and the driver's seat, Promila is seated behind me on the pillion seat with Sharpy in her arms – and, believe it or not – Pramod is seated on the steal carrier at the back. What a scene!

My memories bring me to our once-a-week rigmarole of going to Sector 17 Coffee House for 'badas' and 'dosas'. The chain of memories has another link. The day our eldest Bubby had usurped my place by ordering the bearer of the coffee house: *"Baira, Bill Lao!" (Waiter, please bring the bill.)*...And we were so pleased with this growing prodigy! Another memory of the Coffee House is the two eldest holding their Curree-soiled hands aloft and walking to the bath room behind the cafeteria to wash their hands. I remember that the cafeteria did not provide any paper napkins. Mom took Sharpy to the bathroom herself. So much for the differential treatment for the youngest!

Then there are three photographs, all black-and-white of my Mom. One in mourning for my father who expired ere he was fifty and, five years his junior, she became a widow soon after the partition of the country. The second is at the time of my marriage, a happy, joyous lady in her late fifties, celebrating the occasion, dancing with her daughters and grand-daughters. Oh, God, she doesn't look old at all. The third is terrible reminder of three untoward tragedies that happen to me. There are three ladies in this picture, all of them now no more. One, of course, is my own Mom. The second lady is the Mom of my children. And how can I say anything about the third without wiping a tears flowing on my cheeks? She is my daughter-in-law, Bubby's wife who couldn't see her four children blossoming like so many flowers in the family garden and expired in her youth. So heavy-hearted it left me, indeed, looking at this photograph. All three ladies are now gone forever.

And I put back the old album in the bookshelf, heave a sigh and wipe away a tear or two from my eyes!

*   *   *

BUDDING OF THREE FRAGRANT FLOWERS

A flower, some poet said, is the poetry of reproduction. It is an example of the eternal seduction of life. Well, that's true about children too. Children also are the poetry of reproduction – reproduction not simply of life in general but life in the DNA shrouded life of the mother and the father – and of countless generations of their forefathers and foremothers before.

Do you know that some flowers bud forth very slowly? First one little bud, rounded, button-like appears and it seems that it would take ages to grow forth and become a rounded green marble before it bursts forth in colours of all hues of the spectrum. On the contrary, there are plants that shoot forth their buds almost instantaneously. The little salubrious branch seems quite innocent, and lo and behold, overnight there comes on it a bud that blossoms forth by the evening. Well, Bubby was like that. It took him well nigh first eight or nine, nay even 12 years to be lily-white like pure, angelic, (though not chubby), without a stain or a blemish, like virgin snow – and then, suddenly he became a near-ripe young man with likes and dislikes of his own. Guileless he continued to be, for he never told a blatant lie but, well, sometimes, an occasional untruth and then give an angelic smile to cover it up. That he remained ingénue and naïve in his dealings with boys of his own age was something that he had inherited from me. I myself could never deceive any one at that age, nor I could ever divine that someone else was deceiving me.

Well, Sharpy was a late 'budding innocence'! It took him quite some time to strew the surroundings with his sweet fragrance. That he retains that aura even today when he is a dad himself is also true, but I alone who can see it; others don't. At 5 or 6, trying to look like a piglet, he would make his lips protrude and say, *"Piggy katey ga!"* (The piglet will bite you!)/ And while we all laughed, he joined in the family exhibition of laughter. Daisy, the floweret, clad in a rosy mystery, was also in no hurry to burst forth into a flower. It seemed to both of us that she took as long as five years to finally decide that she must bloom out. When she actually did, she was the cutest of them all: with the cut of her features, her vocal eyes and her build she outshone a thousand girls of her age. Petite, but not tiny or small, even at the tender age of six or seven, she had a promise – the promise of becoming a rosy beauty.

I will continue harping on this tune till my creative harp is satisfied.

*   *   *

OF PERSONS AND PERSONALITIES

MAYA ANGELOU – A
PERSONAL MEMOIRE

A Personal Diary entry dated from 1987

In Southeastern University, Washington D.C., back in 1986, I met a young Afro-Asian teacher who had a not-very-uncommon name, Maya. I told her that Maya was a common name for Hindu girls in India – and – that my mother's sister had this name also. What the word *Maya* meant in Sanskrit was a conundrum for her. So I opened the magic box and told her that among other connotations and denotations, this word meant *illusion* and the visible word was always referred to as *Maya*. "Oh, yes," she said, "now that you tell me, I remember that my poet and singer aunty, who gave me her name at my christening had also told me about its meaning in Hindu mythology."

This is how I got my first introduction to Maya Angelou, through her niece, Maya Gordon, twenty years her junior and a University teacher. She promised to introduce me to her as a fellow poet from India who wrote in four languages, English being one of them – almost like his second mother tongue. The face-to-face introduction came soon after. A poetry collection of mine, titled *Figures of Fantasy,* had been published from New York a few years back. I got an invitation to be present at the annual convention of American booksellers in Washington, D.C. the next year and it was my good fortune that Maya Angelou was to speak and sing as she was one of the senior most featured writers of the time and never missed the convention.

A day before the convention, my young colleague took me to meet her aunty where she was staying – a mid-sized, economy-rated hotel in the town. She shook hands with me and then gave me a warm hug. "So you write in four languages, three of India and one of England....Have you read any of my poems?" I said I had and that I had included two of her poems in my curriculum in Comparative Literature at the senior level. I spoke but little and then I were taken aback when she asked me to *sing* one of my poems in Urdu. "Sing?" I asked her, "I can recite a poem verbatim, but I am no singer, Maya ji." She was rather happy about my using the postfix *ji* with her name but still insisted that I try to sing a poem.

Well, I did use my rusty *trannum* in presenting a poem and she liked it. Then she herself offered, "Let me try my voice..." and she mimicked one of my lines in Urdu in her mellifluous voice. "You have a deep liquid voice, unlike any I have ever heard," I said, "but not well enough for Urdu *ghazal* singing. We in India have *ghazal* singers who excel in their soft, velvety voice, both men and women. "Do they sing their own poetry?" Indeed, I was taken aback. "Yes and No," I said. "Most of these singers are professional play-back ones, but....well, there are some poets, who recite in *tarannum,* that is intone or vocalize in tune ... but others just read out in poetry sessions."

Maya was one year my senior, but when one reaches one's sixties, age doesn't matter. What matters is what you make of your inner age, the *felt age,* to use an adage from Elliot. I started reading her poetry in the right earnest after that. Sometimes I phoned her and she was candid enough to pick up the phone and talk to me. It was a relationship that went ahead in fits and starts for there was hardly anything common between us. Her poetry was altogether different from what I wrote in Urdu, or for that matter, in English, and she was also aware of it. She wrote like she spoke, I wrote like I do not speak at all. *Outward* and *inward,* may be these two words can sum up the difference between us.

Earlier that year, she had the formidable duty of writing and reading a poem for President Bill Clinton's inauguration. She was only the second poet to have the honor, following Robert Frost's appearance for President John F. Kennedy in 1960. If hers was not one of the greatest of poems, it certainly amounted to a grand moment, was my comment to her niece. I added, "Well, if I had been asked by the President of India to write and recite a poem for his inaugural session, I will not be able to do it. I am not that kind of a poet."

"You may write me down in history/ With your bitter, twisted lies," reads a line from one of her most popular poems, "And Still I Rise." "You may trod me in the very dirt/ But still, like dust, I'll rise."

Well, this is the kind of poetry that was in its zenith during the Progressive Writers' Movement in Urdu. I didn't write that kind of poetry then. How could I appreciate it now? But, here was a "black" poet, a glowing symbol of down-trodden people, slaves of yesteryears, and her poetry appealed to their heart more than it did to their intellect...

A native of St. Louis, a child of Arkansas and California, a self-invented and scrappy adventurer in life and, eventually, literature, Angelou spoke directly to the hearts of millions of readers around the globe. In telling her own story in poetry and over the course of a series of memoirs, beginning with "I Know Why the Caged Bird Sings" in 1970, she reflected her readers' wounds and bolstered their dreams.

I met her only once after that when I went to Kansas City to meet an ailing friend. She had, by that time, joined Hallmark in Kansas City, which teamed with her on a line of cards and other products and engaged her in movie projects. It was a five-minute handshake, a warm hug and a few formal questions and equally formal answers – and it left me with a sense of emptiness. So warm a poet in her poetry, so cold in her personal relations? I asked myself.

But was she really cold in her personal relations. Well, her niece agreed with me on that issue. "You see," she said, "Aunty Maya has the artist's erratic mode of behavior. She can be generous, kind, dry with a rasping voice or bubbling with sweetness. It all depends on time and occasion."

I wasn't much of a friend of Maya Angelou but she did remind me many a women poets in the world who succeeded against a male-dominated or a racially disadvantaged society. "Even though most critics argue that autobiographies are not works of literature, Angelou's literary voice was revered for her poetic command and her commitment to civil rights. She lived through the horrors of racism of the southern America, suffered sexual abuse, remained homeless, had to work as a prostitute and a madam for survival and yet developed a spirit to sing Calypso songs. The six-feet tall, warm and spirited Angelou, never allowed the odds against her imposed by a massive, powerful society to diminish her soul..." wrote a columnist.

Well another time and another day, I might look at her work in the real context of American poetry. Where does she stand? Nowhere in the tradition of American poets, would my answer be. Is she going to leave a tradition of her own? Is she a poet's poet? Well, it is time that is going to tell us, but if there are any indications of 'future time' now, the answer would again be negative. No, she has not nurtured any progeny. There are no poets in America today who could be called 'The Maya Angelou tribe'.

*   *   *

A BRUSH WITH JOHN UPDIKE

Around 1985 when I took up a teaching position with the Southeastern University, Washington D.C., I was given an English course that had "*The Norton Anthology of Poetry*" (2182 pages) as the students' textbook. I could choose my course material. Of living American poets, the ones I chose included John Updike. A year junior to me in age, he had given to the corpus of American poetry something that it lacked, namely religious fervor.

A short piece of his that I came across was titled *I MISSED HIS BOOK BUT READ HIS NAME*. It seemed to have been written in a light mood and castigated a common name from South India. Mr. M. Anantanarayanan, a novelist had published his novel "The Silver Pilgrimage" and The New York Times had taken notice of it. John Updike dwelt jocularly upon the unpronounceable name in his poem. Here is the poem in stanza form.

Though authors are a dreadful clan / To be avoided if you can / I'd like to meet the Indian, M. Anantanarayanan. / I picture him as short and tan. / We'd meet, perhaps, in Hindustan. I'd say, with admirable *Elan* / "Ah, Anantanarayanan. / I have heard of you. The *Times* once ran / A notice of your novel, an / Unusual tale of God and Man." / Would seat me on a lush divan / And read his name – that sumptuous span / Of "a"s and "n"s more lovely than / "In Xanadu did Kubla Khan". Aloud to me all day, I plan / Henceforth to be an ardent fan / Of Anantanarayanan -- / Anantanarayanan.

This poem rankled in my mind and I thought I would get even with him by writing my own poem addressed to him. I did, and to top it all, whenever I taught his poem in the classroom, I read out my own poem as well, to the great delight of my students. Well, here is my poem.

TO JOHN UPDIKE

(In response to his poem belittling M. Anantanaraynan)*

John Updike suffers unashamedly
Of dysentery, the ubiquitous result of being
A Caucasian with a twisted tongue, words flowing
From both ends.

What is so difficult man, to pronounce
A hallowed name that means God Almighty?
You call authors 'a dreadful clan
To be avoided if you can.' But Anantanarayanan
You would like to keep confined to Hindustan.

Picture yourself with the man who's a marvel
He 'as short and tan'; you 'as tall and marmoreal'.
And you say you do now plan
to be his life-long ardent fan.

You'd seat him, you say, on a lush divan
More luscious than one in Zanadu of Kubla Khan
And then practice saying again and again
All the "a"s and "n"s together, crazy or sane.

I know, John, you're fond of names
Wigglesworth and Killpatrick and Hughshumphrey
They enter your poems all and sundry
So be at ease, offense is taken anon
By me or by Anantanaryanan.

*The chance to talk to him came pretty late in my life as I got involved in my domestic affairs. However, a couple of years before his death, (He died on January 27, 2009), I left a message with his secretary that I would like to meet him for a few minutes. He called me on phone and said he would be happy to meet a fellow poet from India. The date, time and place were settled. I had to meet him in the office of *The New Yorker,* and from there, he said we would go for a drink and a bite.

Our meeting was a great success. I found him a jocular person, ever ready to laugh. When I referred to his poem, he said that he had read this unpronounceable name in The New York Times and was so given to its nasal twang that he practiced pronouncing it. When he couldn't, he wrote the poem but it was not done to belittle the gentleman whom he had never met. Anyway, I told him that I had written a poem addressed to him. He was intrigued. He told me he had never had anyone write a poem addressed to him. A drink or two later, I read out the poem. He laughed at almost every line of it. When his laughter subsided, he said, "Come on Satyapal, let's have a wager. If you can pronounce the gentleman's name five times without stuttering or stopping, I will give you twenty dollars. If you can't, you will give me fifty." I got the catch. "Don't act the Jew with me, John," I said, "Twenty it is for both of us." He laughed. "All right, let's act Hindu with each other. Twenty it is each way."

It is an interesting story, but the fact of the matter is that I lost the bet. The first two times I succeeded but at the third time I stuttered and lost the momentum to pronounce *Anantanarayanan* in one breath. I would say *Ananta* and then pause for a mini-second before continuing with *Narayanan.* He was happy with himself. He said, "Let me sign your poem so that you have a record that I approved of it." He signed the poem with my pen. I have treasured the piece of paper ever since. Here is his signature on my poem.

THE LAST NAUGHTY PIECE

GAYS AND NOT SO GAYS

Is there any logic for a law in the bedroom? From Greece to Rome to the medieval and modern times in Europe (not so particularly) and Muslim ruled countries (very particularly) what happens in the bedroom was left to the bedroom couples, be they a husband-and-wife duo or any other pair. Although the exception to this rule held sway a lot of times everywhere in the world, none ever thought of the couple being any other than a male and a female.

So did India. India it is, however, that has just legalized same sex unions, an ad hoc situation, into a lawful one. Was it moral? Yes and no! Ms. Shobhini Ghosh, Sajjad Zaheer Professor at the AJK Mass Communication Research Center, Jamia Milia Islamia, Delhi, has recently penned a piece in *Hindustan Times* with the title *End to unnatural exclusion* –, a thought-provoking article that discusses almost every aspect of the problem but stops short of discussing the much-maligned term, 'unnatural'.

What is natural sex? Of course, it is between a man and a woman if it is consensual. This answer excludes Lesbian, Gay, Bisexual and Transgender (LGBT) sex. Article 377 that has continued to hold force since the British days in India and Pakistan has never been revised, much less removed after 1947.

However, its use has been rare and, according to Barrister Iqbal Mirza, less than 0.1 percent cases are registered by the police for forced sodomy of teenage or even younger boys by adults in Pakistan. "Even if a report is lodged," he writes, "the offender is let off by the police with a smirk and a dirty smile or is slapped and asked to refrain from the practice." I dare say that the figures in India would not be less glaring though the practice is more prevalent in North and North Western India. South India, by and large, is free of it.

Some anal-retentive, self-righteous Hindu leaders have come up to say that ancient Indian culture, as culled from literature (both religious and non-religious) of those days, does not refer to same gender sex – and that the practice started after Muslim conquest of India. They never tire of pin-pointing Farsi and Urdu saint-poets' and Sufis' glorification of love for comely boys. Indeed true, but chapter and verse can be quoted about *Ishq-i-Majazi* (Love Corporeal) being the first step for *Ishq-i-Haqeeqi*, (Love Spiritual) and no one would dispute this fact.

In India and Pakistan, *hijras* (both transvestites and hermaphrodites) have existed on the sidelines of the society that sustains them as parasites. Article 377 is a British-made law that applies to both countries. Now that India has got rid of it, there are sporadic voices in Pakistan for amending this law if not effacing it. Pakistan, as we all know, has developed a monochromatic culture in the last 60 years and any departure from it is cannot find favour, particularly if it is prompted by a move from India.

However, it wasn't the case in the fifties of the last century. Majeed Lahori, a *gup-shup* (humorist) columnist in an Urdu daily from Lahore, once wrote a poem about hijras. I still remember two lines from it.

Hijra hoon, hijra hoon, hijra hoon, dosto….Aap se purdah hai kia, aao dikhaun kia hoon main!

(A *hijra* I am, a *hijra* I am, a *hijra* I am, my friends / There's no *purdah (veil)* from you: Come and see what I am!

It is well nigh certain that the twilight zone in which hermaphrodites exist because of the midway point they occupy between male and female of the human species, no one would like to explore that forbidden territory unless one is gay himself or not so gay herself. However we cannot blame them for the generic misfortune they have no control over. Their lifestyle of song and dance and quaint dress for charging their "fee" at happy occasion like marriage or birth of a male baby in a household has held its sway over centuries.

Lastly, are their no hijras in North America? Don't ask me. Ask a renowned Urdu poet who has publicly declared himself as gay. Attaulhaq Qasmi's famous quip about him rings in many people's ears. (I dare not repeat it in this column). However, it is statistically true that about 0.01 per cent babies born here are full or part hermaphrodites and need surgery later in childhood but, throughout their lives, their sexual craving remains for the dominant sex in their mixed up genes.

Are you surprised?

*   *   *

Printed in the United States
By Bookmasters